ISOBEL ARM.
General Edito.

BRYAN LOUGHREY
Advisory Editor

ANNE BRONTË

Anne Brontë

By my daughter Charlotte
J. Brontë Minr

ANNE BRONTË
drawn by Charlotte Brontë, 17 April 1833

WW

ANNE BRONTË

BETTY JAY

Northcote House
in association with the
British Council

© Copyright 2000 by Betty Jay

First published in 2000 by Northcote House Publishers Ltd, Horndon, Tavistock, Devon, PL19 9NQ, United Kingdom.
Tel: +44 (01822) 810066 Fax: +44 (01822) 810034.

British Library Cataloguing in Publication Data
A catalogue record for this book is available from the British Library

ISBN 0-7463-0888-4

Typeset by PDQ Typesetting, Newcastle-under-Lyme
Printed and bound in Great Britain by
The Baskerville Press, Salisbury, Wiltshire, SP1 3UA

In memory of Eddie Rynn

Contents

Acknowledgements

I am grateful to Isobel Armstrong for encouraging me to write on Anne Brontë. Many thanks to Carl Plasa for his help during the preparation of the manuscript.

Biographical Outline

1820   Anne Brontë born (17 January), the sixth and last child of Reverend Patrick Brontë and Maria Brontë née Branwell. The family move to Haworth Parsonage, Yorkshire, where Patrick Brontë takes up his post as perpetual curate.

1821   Death of Anne's mother (15 September).

1825   Deaths of Anne's older sisters, Maria and Elizabeth.

1826   Patrick gives his son, Branwell, a gift of toy soldiers. The children invent stories, plays and poems about these figures. These evolve into the Angria Chronicles of Charlotte and Branwell and the Gondal Saga of Emily and Anne.

1831   Charlotte goes to Roe Head School, Yorkshire.

1832   After less than eighteen months at school Charlotte returns home to take on the role of teacher to Emily and Anne.

1835   Anne goes to Roe Head School.

1837   Anne falls ill at school and suffers a religious crisis. She returns to Haworth.

1839   Anne takes up her first position as governess to the Ingham family at Blake Hall.

1840   William Weightman, with whom Anne is alleged to have been romantically involved, is appointed curate to Patrick Brontë. Anne takes up her second governessing post with the Robinson family at Thorp Green Hall, near York.

1842   William Weightman dies of cholera.

1845   Anne resigns her post at Thorp Green and Branwell is dismissed shortly after from his role as tutor following allegations of an affair with Mrs Robinson.

1846   Charlotte organizes the publication of *Poems* by Currer, Ellis and Acton Bell. It sells two copies.

1847   Publication of *Jane Eyre*, *Agnes Grey* and *Wuthering Heights*.

1848   Publication of *The Tenant of Wildfell Hall*. Death of Branwell (24 September) and Emily (19 December).

1849   Anne Brontë, sick with consumption, visits Scarborough and dies (28 May).

Abbreviations

AG   *Agnes Grey*, ed. with an introduction and notes by Angeline Goreau (London and New York: Penguin, 1988)

CH   Miriam Allott (ed.), *The Brontës: The Critical Heritage* (London and Boston: Routledge and Kegan Paul, 1974)

PAB   *The Poems of Anne Brontë: A New Text and Commentary*, ed. Edward Chitham (London and Basingstoke: Macmillan, 1979). All references to the poems are from this edition.

TWH   *The Tenant of Wildfell Hall*, ed. with an introduction and notes by Stevie Davies (London and New York: Penguin, 1986)

Introduction

Approaches to Anne Brontë

The literary achievement of the Brontë sisters is difficult to disentangle from the powerful set of myths which has grown up around the family over the past one hundred and fifty years. In the case of Anne Brontë this problem is compounded by the fact that she has for so long been overshadowed by her two elder siblings, Emily and Charlotte. This is illustrated by the critical reaction to Anne Brontë's first novel, *Agnes Grey* (1847). First published in tandem with *Wuthering Heights*, it was significantly eclipsed by the controversy generated by Emily's text. At the same time, the subject matter of Anne's first novel, the life of a governess, led to unfavourable comparisons with Charlotte Brontë's *Jane Eyre*, which had appeared only two months before.[1] The tendency among Brontë's contemporary reviewers to evaluate her achievement in terms of that of her sisters has been, equally – until fairly recently – a characteristic of the work of many twentieth-century critics.[2] The habitual recourse to such comparatist approaches is matched only by biographical ones which, in Elizabeth Langland's paraphrase, reinforce Charlotte Brontë's conviction that 'Anne's novels were basically autobiographical'.[3] Yet the problem with criticism which draws on biographical material in relation to Anne is that it only feeds the larger cultural fascination with the lives of the Brontë's without necessarily contributing to an understanding of her work.

While some of the mystery surrounding the identities of Currer, Ellis and Acton Bell was resolved by Charlotte after the deaths of her sisters in 1848 and 1849 respectively, speculation about the Brontës did not end there. How did the daughters of a village clergyman, who lived relatively sheltered lives in Haworth, manage to capture the imagination of the reading public with their novels? What experiences shaped their passionate, often brutal artistic visions? How did these women make such an impact on the male-dominated genre of the novel? These questions have been asked by successive generations of readers drawn as much to the tragedy of the Brontës' short lives as to the literary worlds which they created.

The publication of Elizabeth Gaskell's *The Life of Charlotte Brontë* (1857) satisfied some of the curiosity surrounding the Brontës. It also represented the first instalment of the many which go to create the Brontë myth which contemporary critics must still negotiate. Today, this mythology conjures the image of the reclusive genius of Emily, the frustrated artistry of the self-destructive Branwell and the determination of Charlotte, the only one of the family of writers who survived to enjoy, albeit briefly, the attentions of her literary contemporaries. Indeed, Charlotte's survival of her two sisters provides one clue to the way in which Anne's reputation has been created, for Gaskell reinforced Charlotte's characterization of Anne as 'a very sincere and practical Christian' whose writings were guided by a sense of 'duty'.[4] If Anne's first novel established her reputation as the most moralistic of the three sisters, this view was apparently confirmed by the publication of *The Tenant of Wildfell Hall* (1848). It has, until recently, rarely been contradicted by subsequent critics.[5]

The feminist criticism which emerged in the 1970s has enabled critics to approach Anne's work in ways which differ substantially from previous generations. For example, Langland argues that 'Anne was self-consciously critiquing her sisters' work and establishing alternative standards and values'.[6] Jill L. Matus and Susan Meyer are critics who also challenge the assumption that Brontë's work is relatively simple and predominantly moralistic. In her reading of *Agnes Grey*, Matus foregrounds notions of confession and secrecy as 'the shaping conditions for representing female desire' and eschews reading the text 'as a dispassionate and stoic account of governessing'.[7] Meyer's focus on language and resistance allows her to consider in detail Brontë's exploration of silence and forms of 'verbal repression'[8] in the novel. Like Matus, she sets out to reappraise a

2

writer whose work is 'frequently dismissed in a cursory fashion as less passionate and original than the fiction of her two better-known sisters'.[9] These feminist critics' examination of Brontë's complex engagement with questions of power, oppression and resistance is taken up and developed in the first two chapters of this book.

As a contribution to the governess debates of the early to mid Victorian era, *Agnes Grey* offers a detailed account of the daily struggles of the governess as she tries to establish a place for herself in a society where she, by virtue of her class and gender, is consistently devalued. Along with its concern for the injustices faced by the middle-class working woman, the novel offers a perceptive analysis of the many power relations which operate within Victorian society. Relationships between parents and children, employers and employees, men and women, as well as between the different classes, are all represented in this text. As it explores these relationships, the novel demonstrates the extent to which Victorian ideologies of gender and class permeate every aspect of life. *Note well.*

Far too easily dismissed as a text bound by both autobiographical conventions and its reformist agenda, *Agnes Grey* is careful not only to delineate the hierarchies which govern patriarchal society but to explore the possible ways in which these can be challenged. Agnes's own attempts to resist injustice and oppression are based upon firm Christian principles but, given her relative disempowerment, are not always enough to bring about change or triumph. Often forced to collude with the power structures she despises, Agnes is made to compromise her principles in order to function within a society and culture which have little regard for the governess.

The way in which Brontë addresses the question of power in *Agnes Grey* extends beyond an analysis of the condition of the governess and the resources upon which she must draw in order to negotiate the forces which oppress her. Through its focus on education and the processes which produce the gendered subject, the novel equally foregrounds the place of the child within culture and society. Refusing to idealize childhood, *Agnes Grey* insists that the children placed in Agnes's care are, like their governess, equally caught up in the power structures which determine class and gender roles. The ways in which these children and adolescents deal with the expectations placed upon them, often by exploiting their class status and the roles they are assigned within a patriarchal society, is one of the most fascinating aspects of Brontë's text, and no less compelling than its account of the conflicts which beset their governess.

Brontë's willingness to draw upon her own experiences as a governess in the novel suggests that one of her concerns is to break down the private/public distinctions which demarcate what aspects of existence could legitimately be the focus of a socially engaged literature. Such a dismantling of these distinctions becomes even more pronounced in *The Tenant*, Brontë's second novel. In this epistolary text, Brontë experiments with perspective and the conventions of linear plot to produce a narrative structure as complex as that which has so exercised critics of *Wuthering Heights*. Focusing on the woman's story as it is passed between men, the novel demonstrates from the outset Brontë's awareness of the power of language in its written and spoken forms, as well as the way in which it may be appropriated.

The subject matter of *The Tenant* is no less radical than the form in which it is presented. The novel delves beneath the surface of respectable Victorian life in order to expose to public scrutiny the tyranny inflicted upon a woman who is trapped in a domestic nightmare. By revealing the terrors to which Helen Huntington is exposed by her husband and his degenerate cohorts, Brontë breaks through the silence which enshrouds the marital experience. As a study in the abuse of power, the novel offers Brontë's readers the opportunity to explore female disempowerment within a patriarchal society and represents a thoroughgoing indictment of that society, its culture and laws. From Helen's first romantic aspirations to her flight from tyranny and attempts to live an independent life, the novel insists on forging connections between the individual and the ideology which informs and shapes every level of experience. It offers a complex account of the networks of power which operate within the domestic and familial realms. An understanding of these networks is not only crucial to the development of Brontë's heroine as she begins to resist her own victimization, but also underscores the novel as a whole.

While Brontë's two novels provide plenty of scope for an interrogation of her political agenda through an analysis of the social and cultural structures which operate within the texts, her poetry represents more of a challenge to the reader. Conventionally divided into devotional poetry and love lyrics these verses, which number more than sixty in total, appear at first glance simply to endorse a traditional poetic language. Articulating the tensions between faith and doubt, duty and will, human desire and the wish for transcendence, love and loss, these writings cover a ground which is familiar to readers of nineteenth-century poetry. At the same time, Brontë's verse proves to be deceptive in terms of both its language and form. It demands that the reader attend to Brontë's own awareness of poetic conventions and tropes in order to trace, through the practice of close and careful reading, the processes which enable her to subvert these conventions. In this way, the simple surfaces of the verse can be exposed to reveal the intensity of Brontë's interrogation of language and subjectivity. As it explores the many facets of the spiritual, sexual and always questioning subject, Brontë's poetry has much to offer the reader of today wishing to understand the female poetic tradition and the development of Victorian poetry alike. To underestimate Brontë's contribution to the novel and to the poetic form is to collude with a literary and critical history which has had so little time for the youngest Brontë sister and which has, for far too long, left assumptions about her writing to go unchallenged. Those who approach Brontë's work with an awareness of recent theoretical debates concerning feminism, subjectivity, power and agency, and with the spirit of critical inquiry which characterizes her poetry, will quickly understand that she has much to offer.

1

Governing Desires in *Agnes Grey*

All true histories contain instruction; though, in some, the treasure may be hard to find, and when found, so trivial in quantity that the dry, shrivelled kernel scarcely compensates for the trouble of cracking the nut. (*AG* 61)

THE GOVERNESS DEBATES

Given its central focus on the governess figure, *Agnes Grey* is necessarily implicated in larger contemporary debates concerning the problems of governessing. These debates were not only conducted within the magazines and journals which circulated at the time, but were also, in the latter half of the nineteenth century, rehearsed within the context of increasingly popular governess novels.[1] Brontë's own governess's tale represents one of the first of the many texts which detail the conditions in which growing numbers of middle-class Victorian women laboured.[2] For some commentators, the nineteenth-century concern for the plight of the governess 'seems somewhat excessive',[3] particularly when one considers the high incidence of women employed in domestic service or in industry. Yet the attention afforded to the governess not only signals a middle-class bias on the part of philanthropists and social commentators but is also symptomatic of the multiple anxieties – relating to class, work, education and gender – to which her existence gives rise.

The fact that middle-class, educated women found themselves in need of paid employment signalled the economic instability of their class, which later historians in part ascribe to the increasing numbers of single eligible men who sought their fortunes in the colonies. Given a social and cultural milieu in which female confinement in the home was seen to be a sign of success, employment as a governess placed the daughters of the financially stricken middle classes in a compromising as well as compromised position, even as paid work within the home – albeit the home of another – was seen to be less invidious than other forms of employment. It enabled the governess to retain her connections with her own class and to carry out duties which in other circumstances she might have performed for her own children.[4] Despite the 'undoubted merit of domesticity',[5] the installation of the governess in the home of her middle-class employers was not an entirely comfortable arrangement. Although her status as 'gentlewoman' was precisely what fitted her for the role of educator, her financial insecurity was the index of a 'fallen' economic condition and so considerably diminished her status. A 'gentlewoman' obliged to work for a living as a governess was, while not exactly reduced to the servant class, no longer her employers' equal:

> She was hired to provide the children, and particularly the young women of the family, with an education to prepare them for leisured gentility. But she had been educated in the same way, and for the same purpose, and her employment became a prostitution of her education, of the values underlying it, and of her family's intentions in providing it. Her function as a status symbol of middle-class gentility also perverted her own upbringing.[6]

Given the problematic status of the governess, it is clear that the debates surrounding her extend beyond a concern with the conditions in which middle-class women laboured, or the fact that they were forced to work at all. The plight of the governess was also the plight of those whose education depended upon her skills. The often unsatisfactory quality of the teaching provided by governesses who were themselves poorly educated added another dimension to the demand, not only for formal female education, but also for an education which more closely resembled that which was available to boys.[7] These issues, already powerfully addressed in the eighteenth century by Mary Wollstonecraft's *Vindication of the Rights of Woman* (1792), are also dramatized in Brontë's text. Agnes Grey's responsibilities vary according to the sex of her pupils, and much of the text is devoted to the education she is expected to provide for the girls given over to her care. These reluctant female charges are expected to attain only the rudiments of a formal education while devoting their energies to the pursuit of more superficial 'accomplishments' designed to attract future husbands and, in this way, they live out a fate which calls into question the politics and ethics of a gendered education system.

Agnes Grey addresses many of the anxieties underpinning the governess debates and as such can be seen as socially and politically engaged. It details the difficult conditions under which the governess labours and which are accentuated by her lack of social status and disempowerment within home and community alike. The novel is marked by an equally important emphasis on the ideological function of education as it relates not only to class but also gender. This double focus on the construction and perpetuation of particular power relations within the familial or domestic setting is extended to include an analysis of the hierarchies which operate within society at large. In this respect, the text's preoccupation with the governess-figure enables Brontë to move beyond the confines of the school-room to provide a critique of oppressive forces within the wider world.

'REVERSING THE ORDER OF THINGS'

In the opening paragraph of her narrative, Agnes Grey suggests that the story she will relate has a dual potential insofar as it 'might prove useful to some, and entertaining to others'. Inviting the reader to share in a narrative which she would not otherwise 'disclose to the most intimate friend', Agnes at the same time downplays the complexity of the text. While participating in contemporary debates about education and the condition of the governess, the novel not only critiques class and gender relations but also incorporates into its 'true histor[y]' (*AG* 61) an account of the romantic career of its narrator. Although the novel's usefulness may seem to be limited to its concern with social issues, Agnes does not, in her opening address, suggest that this is exclusively the case. This leaves open the possibility that the romance element in the novel itself has a certain heuristic value.[8] As the narrative unfolds, it becomes clear that the 'Art of Instruction' to which it alludes (in the title to chapter two) relates as much to the experience of desire as the vocation of the governess.

'The Art of Instruction' succinctly captures the novel's status as a depiction of many different forms of learning. Education is certainly one of the keys to the text in terms of Agnes's professional role but also important because Agnes's subjective experience as educator equally constitutes a process of instruction which she, in turn, relays to the reader. In her account of the instructional aims of *Agnes Grey*, Langland notes that the novel intends 'to keep the reader focussed on the life of a mind'.[9] Though the 'life of a mind' is important in the text, it is not left unchallenged by the conflicts which arise when passion disrupts the principles of reason and religion that typically govern Agnes's interactions with others. As Matus argues, critics who have interpreted *Agnes Grey* as a 'narrative of growth and maturation, unusual in allowing its female protagonist independence' have been less likely to 'read it as a novel of intense passions, concerned with competition and triumph, and meditating on the mysterious and perplexing nature of sexual attraction'.[10] Although Agnes's own passion surfaces in the violence with which she is forced to deal with the children in her charge, it is only in the latter half of the novel that a different kind of passion – associated with sexual desire – calls into doubt the very standards which sustain Agnes during her governessing trials. As her narrative makes the transition from social critique to romance, it is not only her reasoning which falters but also her Christian piety. Since reason and Christian values constitute the foundations of Agnes's own resistance to the power structures in which she is enmeshed, the sexual desire she experiences both precipitates a personal and spiritual crisis and forces the reader to re-esteem the social critique the narrative initially offers. In this way, the tensions which arise in the textual shift to romance further refine and revise the instructional goals of the novel.

Agnes Grey offers its readers an account of the career and courtship of its eponymous narrator which crucially focuses attention on the ways in which power is organized and sustained within a patriarchal society. From the outset, the text concerns itself with the many forms of power Agnes must

9

negotiate. It delineates the first of the hierarchies in which the narrator is embedded with an account of the dynamics which operate within Agnes's own family and form the impetus for her to seek employment. The youngest daughter of a clergyman, Agnes is frustrated by a family which consistently infantilizes her. The designated 'child, and the pet of the family', Agnes exists in a condition of enforced immaturity, rendered 'by ceaseless kindness...too helpless and dependent, too unfit for buffeting with the cares and turmoils of life' (*AG* 62). Although she insists that her parents enjoy a loving and respectful relationship, it is her father's attempts to improve their financial circumstances, and the life of the woman who has married him for love and against her family's wishes, which decimate the already limited family fortune. His investments lost in a shipwreck, Agnes's father does not recover from his failed speculations and subsequently suffers a decline. In contrast to her brooding sister Mary, Agnes views the family misfortunes as a challenge for, she says, 'there was something exhilarating in the idea of being driven to straits, and thrown upon our own resources' (*AG* 64). Yet Agnes's enthusiasm for household chores (with the departure of the servants) cannot be translated into action because both mother and sister underestimate her abilities. Insisting that she is 'a woman in [her] own estimation' (*AG* 66), the 18-year-old Agnes consequently announces her wish to assist her family by taking up a place as governess. This proposition meets with incredulity from her mother, who declares, 'you have not learned to take care of *yourself* yet', and a sister who cautions Agnes against a course which would place her 'in a house full of strangers, without me or mamma to speak and act for you...with a parcel of children, besides yourself, to attend to; and no one to look to for advice' (*AG* 68). Agnes's own recollection of these family exchanges, in which her mother designates her a 'naughty girl' (*AG* 69) and her sister comments that as a governess '[She] would not even know what clothes to put on' (*AG* 68), suggests that she seeks to empower herself by gaining independence and, equally, by proving her family wrong. She summarizes the benefits of becoming a governess as follows:

> To go out into the world; to enter upon a new life; to act for myself; to exercise my unused faculties; to try my unknown powers; to earn my own maintenance... to show papa what his little Agnes could do;

to convince mamma and Mary that I was not quite the helpless, thoughtless being they supposed. (*AG* 69)

To the fantasy of autonomy projected here is added the 'inducement' of Agnes's idealized notion of the governess's role. Agnes's coming-of-age is subsequently traced by the text through her placement with two families, the Bloomfields and the Murrays. In the first of these, her charges are 7-year-old Tom and his sister, Mary Ann, aged 6. In the second family the children are adolescent. Agnes's own growth is mirrored by the development of the children for whom she is responsible so that she comes to maturity alongside Rosalie, the eldest child of the second family, with whom she will compete romantically.

For Langland, *Agnes Grey* operates as a female version of the male *bildungsroman*. Instead of the hero's 'two love affairs, one sexual and one spiritual',[11] Brontë places Agnes in relation to children who challenge her, first physically and then spiritually. In this way the conventions of a male genre are adapted to suit the development of a female protagonist. Yet this process seems to produce less definitive results than Langland suggests. When confronting the Bloomfield children – particularly Tom – Agnes must learn to resist the violence of male sexuality and the abuse of power, just as the behaviour of Rosalie forces Agnes to confront and compete against a manipulative female sexuality. Within both families Agnes is pitted against different and gendered forms of sexuality and power. Her sense of spiritual superiority, as the pious and well-informed clergyman's daughter, is constantly threatened by her ineffectual interventions in the Bloomfield family, her failure to teach the children and convince the parents of their own failings. The spiritual resources upon which she draws in her dealings with the Bloomfields sustain her throughout her early trials with this family but are significantly compromised, if not wholly undermined, when Agnes is in her second placement and must negotiate her desire for the curate, Mr Weston.

Here, Agnes's struggles against ideologies of class and gender become increasingly personalized. Her lowly status as governess casts doubt on her value as a potential spouse, particularly when she is measured against the wealthy and attractive Rosalie. Unwilling to adopt Rosalie's flirtatious and manipulative femininity, Agnes relies on the sense of order and righteousness her spiritual faith bestows, but increasingly doubts whether these principles will prevail in more worldly contexts. At the same time, Agnes's own sexual desire for Weston disrupts the spirituality to which she clings and stoicism to which it gives rise. Her devotions become infused with less than spiritual longings for the curate. Forced to admit both the affects of her own desires and the possibility that they may be thwarted, she seeks to re-establish the equilibrium which existed before Weston's appearance and to transcend her own needs as a woman. The acknowledgement and subsequent repression of desire eventually comes to dominate Agnes's narrative. Lacking both economic status and sexual allure, she struggles to reconcile herself to the prospect of spinsterhood by repudiating her desires.

Upon securing her first post Agnes quickly learns that her declaration of independence as 'a woman in [her] own estimation' is undercut by the sexual and class politics which operate within the Bloomfield family. Leaving behind the protections of home, she enters a context in which she, as 'woman' and employee, is doubly disempowered. The Bloom-fields elevate the children above the governess by virtue of a class status only recently attained through trade (the mercantile origins of the family are marked by the description of their home as 'the new but stately mansion of Wellwood', *AG* 73). Witness to Mr Bloomfield's petty tyrannies and completely devalued by both parents, Agnes must labour under a system within which she is denied the 'privilege' of either rewarding or punishing her charges. Instead of bribery and threats she must discover other ways in which to negotiate the rebellious children who inherit their parents' class bias and for whom 'The name of governess...was a mere mockery' (*AG* 84). Their delight in 'reversing the order of things' (*AG* 81) is sanctioned by a family which has no respect for the lowly governess.

Agnes provides a detailed but edited account of her dealings with the Bloomfields, 'for fear', she says, 'of trespassing too much upon the reader's patience'. She further justifies her narration of events by claiming that her 'design...was not to amuse, but to benefit those whom it might concern'. Included amongst such imagined beneficiaries are the parents of young children as well as any 'unfortunate governess' (*AG* 93). Agnes's account of her school-room trials extends beyond the dramatic rendition of her relationship with the children, although this aspect of the text and, in particular, Agnes's own treatment of the children, deserves critical scrutiny. The narrative offers a complex account of the operations of different forms of power and modes of resistance to it. This power-play relates as much to the behaviour of the children as to Agnes's response to it.[12]

Faced with the 'task of instruction and surveillance' (*AG* 84), Agnes begins by trying to befriend the children and, especially, to appease and 'indulge' (*AG* 77) Tom. This psychological strategy, even coupled with moral and religious guidance, consistently and spectacularly fails. Locked into a battle of wills with Tom and Mary Ann, Agnes participates in a struggle in which her 'unknown powers' manifest themselves through an escalating violence. Agnes's account of this struggle not only constitutes a compelling record of adult disempowerment in an increasingly hostile environment, but also highlights the extent to which the behaviour of both children is informed by the workings of a gendered ideology. In the course of resisting the destructive effects of this ideology, Agnes is ironically forced to appropriate the violence she otherwise associates with masculinity and patriarchal control.

When first introduced to the children, Agnes notes how the boy 'claimed all [her] attention' along with possession of the 'school-room' and 'nice new books'. Their first meeting sees the young master 'stood bolt upright' between Agnes and the fire, 'with his hands behind his back, talking away like an orator, occasionally interrupting his discourse with a sharp reproof to his sisters when they made too much noise'. Agnes's first impressions of the boy given such 'a favourable character by his mamma' (*AG* 76) are confirmed by the child's play with his rocking-horse when, 'ordering his sister to hold the reigns, he mounted, and made [Agnes] stand for ten minutes, watching how manfully he used his whip and spurs'. The display of male violence to which Agnes is here treated is not simply confined to Tom's play-acting, for he insists that he is also 'obliged' to strike his errant sister 'now and then to keep her in order' (*AG* 77). The early intimations of the power-struggle between Tom and Agnes, which will subsequently consume the governess, come on the first day she spends in his company. Tom's guided tour of the grounds of the house takes in his garden along with the extensive traps for birds and animals he has set in order to pursue his vile experiments. Although Agnes's attempts to appeal to Tom's Christian humanity patently fail to sway a boy encouraged in his activities by both parents and uncle, Agnes sets herself against them all when she tells herself that she will resist the slaughter 'as long as [she has] power to prevent it' (*AG* 79). In relation to Tom, it is clear that Agnes is fighting a war against the excesses of patriarchy: 'Master Tom, not content with refusing to be ruled, must needs set up as a ruler, and manifested a determination to keep, not only his sisters, but his governess in order, by violent manual and pedal applications; and, as he was a tall, strong boy of his years, this occasioned no trifling inconvenience.' Resisting the temptation of 'A few sound boxes on the ear' (*AG* 84) for fear of the stories Tom might tell to his mother, rather than because she is forbidden to strike the children, Agnes is obliged to adopt other methods of control. As she comments, 'my only resource was to throw him on his back, and hold his hands and feet till the frenzy was somewhat abated'. Her attempts at physical restraint (which include barricading the children into the school-room) depend not only on strength and stamina but also 'Patience, Firmness, and Perseverence', traits which she describes as her 'only weapons' (*AG* 85) in an unequal fight. As she tries to counter those hierarchies based on gender, class and status within the family which place her in an inferior position, Agnes asserts the superiority which comes with spiritual, moral and intellectual enlightenment. While this alternative hierarchy helps sustain Agnes's morale throughout the duration of her struggle it serves no practical function when it comes to educating the anarchic children. It becomes increasingly clear that Agnes's job requires her to engage more in physical than mental labours. As she notes, 'The task of instruction was as arduous for the body as the mind. I had to run after my pupils to catch them, to carry, or drag them to the table, and often forcibly to hold them there, till the lesson was done' (*AG* 86). This state of affairs calls into question Agnes's position as a woman within the market-place since the more elevated intellectual role she is meant to fulfil is reduced to physical toil and exertion.

The problem of managing Tom and Mary Ann seems to call forth different responses from Agnes. She seeks to curtail the exaggerated masculinity of Tom, 'the little tyrant' (*AG* 104), which has flourished under his mother's devotions and the influence of the men in the household. She claims, however, that despite his violence, Tom proves to be 'by no means the most unmanageable' of the children. Unlike his sister, he sometimes has 'the sense to see that his wisest policy was to finish his tasks', if only in order to escape the confines of the school-room and attentions of the governess. The less rational of the children,· Mary Ann, also displays an apparently unlimited amount of 'obstinacy' in her dealings with Agnes. She forces Agnes into 'a trial of strength...in which [Mary Ann] generally came off victorious; and every victory served to encourage and strengthen her for a future contest' (*AG* 87):

> In vain I argued, coaxed, entreated, threatened, scolded; in vain I kept her in from play, or, if obliged to take her out, refused to play with her, or to speak kindly, or have anything to do with her; in vain I tried to set before her the advantages of doing as she was bid, and being loved and kindly treated in consequence, and the disadvantages of persisting in her absurd perversity. (*AG* 87–8)

Significantly, Mary Ann's resistance to Agnes, here characterised as 'perversity', does not, as is the case with Tom, involve physical assaults on the governess. She more frequently resorts to a form of passive resistance:

> She apparently preferred rolling on the floor to any other amusement. Down she would drop like a leaden weight; and when I, with great difficulty, had succeeded in rooting her thence, I had still to hold her up with one arm, while, with the other, I held the book from which she was to read or spell her lesson. As the dead weight of the big girl of six became too heavy for one arm to bear, I transferred it to the other; or, if both were weary of the burden, I carried her into a corner, and told her she might come out when she could find the use of her feet, and stand up; but she generally preferred lying there like a log till dinner or tea time, when, as I could not deprive her of her meals, she must be liberated, and would come crawling out with a grin of triumph on her round, red face. (*AG* 87)

Although Agnes underlines the extent to which the behaviour of the children is conditioned by gendered ideologies, her

15

dealings with Mary Ann are complicated by an initial assumption that there must be some resemblance between herself and the girl. Such an identification turns out, however, to be wrong, for, as Agnes says: 'With me, at her age, or under, neglect and disgrace were the most dreadful punishments; but on her they made no impression' (AG 88). In relation to the girl, Agnes seems to display an ambivalence which relates to the issue of femininity. Agnes is herself obliged to assist with 'the dressing of Mary Ann', a task which involves preparing her 'abundant hair' with pomade, plaits and bows and which Agnes's 'unaccustomed fingers found great difficulty in performing'. While Agnes here underscores the exaggerated feminine appearance of the girl, she does not associate Mary Ann's 'constant fidget of impatience' (AG 81) with a refusal of the femininity she is obliged to display. Rather, she construes it as an attempt to render the task of governessing more difficult, effectively ignoring an ambivalence which is elsewhere suggested by her own account of Mary Ann's behaviour: 'at one time she would not be washed; at another she would not be dressed, unless she might wear some particular frock that, I knew, her mother would not like her to have; at another she would scream and run away if I attempted to touch her hair' (AG 90). Reading Mary Ann's disruptions as a personal attack on herself, Agnes fails to acknowledge the girl's sporadic attempts to resist an enforced femininity. In this respect, the governess shows the limits of her own analysis of the relationship between gender, power and socialization. She is far more attuned to the implications of Tom's proto-typically patriarchal behaviour than Mary Ann's ambivalence towards conventional notions of femininity and her attempts to resist them.

At other times Agnes constructs Mary Ann in terms of a flawed or excessive femininity and relates this to the pernicious influence of Uncle Robson. In her dealings with the girl, she seeks to extirpate a femininity encouraged by a man for whom, as Agnes explains:

> Mary Ann was something of a favourite. He was continually encouraging her tendency to affectation (which I had done my utmost to crush) talking about her pretty face, and filling her head with all manner of conceited notions concerning her personal appearance (which I had instructed her to regard as dust in the

(handwritten annotation: 2 feminism)

balance compared with the cultivation of her mind and manners); and I never saw a child so susceptible of flattery as she was. (*AG* 102)

Perceiving the narcissism to which Robson's attentions give rise, Agnes seeks to substitute 'mind and manners' for 'conceit' and so to eradicate the distinctly feminine failings of the child. When she makes no impression on Mary Ann, she resorts to physical force and a violence which, significantly, does not manifest itself in her dealings with Tom:

> Sometimes, exasperated to the utmost pitch, I would shake her violently by the shoulders, or pull her long hair, or put her in the corner, – for which she punished me with loud, shrill, piercing screams, that went through my head like a knife. She knew I hated this, and when she had shrieked her utmost, would look into my face with an air of vindictive satisfaction. (*AG* 88)

If the punisher is herself punished here, this is another way in which the 'order of things' in the school-room is reversed. The additional reversal is that the very means with which Agnes strives to regulate Mary Ann's femininity identifies her with the masculine violence she seeks also to curtail in Tom. In appropriating a violent form of control in this way, Agnes can be seen to compromise her own femininity and call into question the principles upon which she bases her criticisms of the little patriarch-in-waiting, Tom.

Tom, like Agnes, practises his own reversals and shows himself, should the need arise, able to enact a feminine form of resistance. This is indicated by one of the exchanges between them. When he realizes that he is physically unable to overcome the governess, Tom twists 'his body and face into the most grotesque and singular contortions' while 'uttering loud yells and doleful outcries, intended to represent weeping, but wholly without the accompaniment of tears'. By relinquishing a masculinity proved impotent and replacing it with feminine affection, Tom adopts a strategy which reverses the conventional gender roles. This strategy is in turn mirrored by Agnes who, confronted by such a spectacle, 'tremble[s] with impatience and irritation' but nonetheless 'manfully' strives 'to suppress all visible signs of molestation, and affect[s] to sit, with calm indifference, waiting till it should please [Tom] to cease this pastime' (*AG* 86). If Tom fakes the behaviour of a distressed child or female hysteric, Agnes's attempts to mask her own responses with masculine 'indifference' equally suggest that the lines which demarcate conventional gendered identities are less rigid than one might suppose.

In the most dramatic of the confrontations between governess and child, Agnes pre-empts Tom's anticipated torture of a nest of baby birds by herself crushing them underneath a stone. Agnes's thwarting of Tom's potential sadism is also a means of resisting the destructive effects of Robson, a man whose interference undercuts her 'whole elaborate course of reasoning and persuasion' (*AG* 103). In her description of Robson, Agnes is careful to highlight the contradictory masculinity he represents. She notes that 'he had found some means of compressing his waist into a remarkably small compass, and that, together with the unnatural stiffness of his form, showed that the lofty-minded, manly Mr Robson, the scorner of the female sex, was not above the foppery of stays' (*AG* 102). While Agnes calls into question Robson's masculinity, she also underlines the sexual power-struggle in which she is forced to engage. Robson, for his part, identifies 'the violence of his nephew's passion' when he is thwarted by Agnes as a sign that he is 'beyond petticoat government already'. If Robson perceives Tom's behaviour as a natural and inevitable form of masculine protest against 'mother, granny, governess, and all!' (*AG* 105), Agnes's own description of Tom's excited possession of the helpless birds is couched in distinctly sexual terms:

> 'They're all mine. Uncle Robson gave them to me – one, two, three, four, five – you shan't touch one of them! no, not one, for your lives!' continued he, exultantly, laying the nest on the ground and standing over it with his legs wide apart, his hands thrust into his breeches-pockets, his body bent forward, and his face twisted into all manner of contortions in the ecstacy of his delight. (*AG* 104)

In this passage, Agnes perceives the sexual origin of Tom's sadism as he asserts his possession of the birds, along with his right to determine their destruction. This in turn suggests that the familial culture in which he flourishes is one which indulges even the most destructive of male desires. In the light of Agnes's ongoing battle to curb these desires, Tom's gleeful anticipation of the death he will bring is no less an attack on Agnes and the principle of nurturance for which she, as woman stands, than Robson's scathing dismissal of the dictates of 'petticoat government' (*AG* 105). Here Agnes's description of Tom's warped face and body echoes the earlier passage in which she endures Tom's 'molestation' without showing outward signs of distress. Agnes's response on this occasion again suggests that she assumes the power associated with patriarchy – this time forestalling Tom's violence rather than adopting a stoical male pose. Although she temporarily frustrates Tom's violent – and somewhat masturbatory – sexuality in the garden scene, she must subsequently defend her actions to Mrs Bloomfield, who perceives Agnes's 'killing [of] the poor birds by wholesale, in that shocking manner' to be an attack on the refined sensibilities of her son. Although the subsequent theological debate between governess and mother demonstrates the scriptural knowledge of both women as they pitch biblical verses at one another, it is clear that Agnes can only participate guardedly in the debate. Her position as governess curtails her ability to resist Mrs Bloomfield's theological assumptions and ensures that her own interpretations of biblical edicts go unvoiced. The scriptural exchange only serves to highlight the extent to which Agnes must suppress her religious convictions when confronted by secular forms of authority. Her integrity, already compromised by the masculine violence with which she attempts to discipline the Bloomfield children, is further eroded.

If Agnes's duties as governess frequently involve physical combat with the children, the need to control their bodies – in order to teach them as well as to avoid the unwanted interference of the parents – extends beyond the school-room. The children's attempts to escape their confinement and the havoc they wreak in the garden bring Agnes's failings to the attention of their father, whereas the impropriety of their behaviour, when confronted with family guests, draws the attention of their mother. The public performances of Tom and Mary Ann are couched in terms which suggest sexual transgression:

> every visitor disturbed me, more or less, not so much because they neglected me (though I did feel their conduct strange and disagreeable in that respect), as because I found it impossible to keep my charges away from them, as I was repeatedly desired to do:

Tom must talk to them, and Mary Ann must be noticed by them. Neither the one nor the other knew what it was to feel any degree of shame-facedness, or even common modesty. They would indecently and clamorously interrupt the conversation of their elders, teaze them with the most impertinent questions, roughly collar the gentlemen, climb their knees uninvited, hang about their shoulders or rifle their pockets, pull the ladies' gowns, disorder their hair, tumble their collars, and importunately beg for their trinkets. (*AG* 106)

The powerlessness of the governess is compounded by Agnes's perception of her own lack of appeal on such occasions. The 'honest words' she insists upon uttering to the children must compete with the flattery and indulgence of the guests, but so too must the 'homely garments' and 'every-day face' which characterize her appearance. Contending against 'the guests, with their fine clothes and new faces' for the attentions of the wayward children, Agnes is unable to 'reach them' (*AG* 106). Her attribution of this failure to a lack of physical appeal as well as social status introduces into the narrative an increasing self-consciousness on Agnes's part with regard to the qualities she can offer the world. At the same time, the clearly sexual language of the passage cited above suggests that this failure is grounded in a lack of seductive power on her part.

THE GOVERNESS IN LOVE

'Seasoned by adversity, and tutored by experience' by the time she receives her notice from the Bloomfields, Agnes nonetheless seeks to compensate for the loss of 'honour in the eyes of those whose opinion was more than that of all the world to [her]' (*AG* 108). Her resources replenished by the 'liberty and rest' (*AG* 109) of a brief sojourn at home, Agnes seeks once again to make her way in the world. When she achieves her second placement, with the Murrays, and finds herself vying for the attentions of Weston, Agnes's sense of her own inadequacy becomes more acute. As the narrative develops, Agnes's spiritual values are called into question by the passion she experiences. Doubting her own worth to a potential suitor, she responds uneasily to the sexual desire she experiences, trying to justify the intensity of her longing by recalling the years of neglect she has endured.

She eventually admits her growing passion for Weston as a legitimate concern by claiming that it arises out of both a human need for social recognition and the desire to encounter a soul whose spiritual outlook reflects her own. In this way, sexual desire is uneasily integrated into the system of social and spiritual values which have hitherto governed Agnes's interactions with others.

Agnes's placement in the Murray household develops some of the concerns of the earlier part of the narrative. Rosalie and her younger sister Matilda can be seen to represent traits which coexist in Mary Ann: one is associated with a manipulative femininity which the other resists. Charged with the care of the adolescent girls, Agnes's duties relate less to the inculcation of knowledge and more to the development of accomplishments. The son and heir of the household, who is 'boisterous, unruly, unprincipled, untaught, unteachable' (*AG* 124), is quickly dispatched to school where his ignorance, Agnes is sure, will 'be laid to the account of his education having been entrusted to an ignorant female teacher, who had presumed to take in hand what she was wholly incompetent to perform' (*AG* 125). Agnes is clearly aware of the assumption that women are less intellectually able than men, but her narrative passes over this aspect of the governess debate. Instead, it focuses on the education of girls. Mrs Murray, who supervises Agnes's duties from afar, wishes the 16-year-old Rosalie and her younger sister to be rendered 'as superficially attractive and showily accomplished as they could possibly be made, without present trouble [or] discomfort to themselves'. Agnes must therefore 'strive to amuse and oblige, instruct, refine, and polish' (*AG* 120) these girls in order to give them the advantage upon their entrance into the marriage-market. Agnes's earlier sexual power-struggles at the Bloomfields' take on a different complexion in this section of the novel. Rosalie's physical assets, her 'form and face' are not matched by her 'mind and disposition' (*AG* 121) and it is this imbalance which Agnes seeks to correct:

> she had never been properly taught the distinction between right and wrong; she had, like her brothers and sisters, been suffered from infancy to tyrannize over nurses, governesses, and servants; she had not been taught to moderate her desires, to control her temper or bridle her will, or to sacrifice her own pleasure for the good of

21

others...her mind had never been cultivated: her intellect at best was somewhat shallow. (AG 122)

If Rosalie presents the acceptable face of conventional feminin-ity, her sister Matilda appears to resist all outward manifesta-tions of decorum and charm. Agnes describes her as 'a veritable hoyden, of whom little need be said' (AG 123). Indifferent to the dictates of the highly regulated femininity she is supposed to embody, Matilda transgresses conventions of gender both physically and verbally. Her preference for the male pursuits of riding and hunting and her propensity to swear 'like a trooper' (AG 124), set her apart from the superficially genteel Rosalie. Like the Bloomfield children, Matilda is described in animalistic terms by Agnes:

> As an animal, Matilda was all right, full of life, vigour, and activity; as an intelligent being, she was barbarously ignorant, indocile, careless, and irrational, and consequently very distressing to one who had the task of cultivating her understanding, reforming her manners, and aiding her to acquire those ornamental attainments which, unlike her sister, she despised as much as the rest. (AG 124)

In contrast to Tom and Mary Ann, who Agnes wishes to see 'become more humanized' (AG 91), Matilda represents a different sort of challenge. Despite Mrs Murray's wishes, Agnes refuses to 'try to form her tastes, and endeavour to rouse and cherish her dormant vanity' by using 'skilful flattery' (AG 124), thus refusing to deploy typically feminine tactics as a means of cultivating the recalcitrant femininity of the girl. In relation to Rosalie, Agnes's own resistance to her version of femininity operates not as a refusal actively to promote the values upheld by Mrs Murray but more in terms of a constant barrage of verbal reproof and correction. Taking an active interest in Rosalie's womanhood, Agnes seems more aware of the purpose behind the ideological formations it is supposed to support. In this part of her narrative Agnes shows a heightened degree of social awareness both with regard to the fate which awaits Rosalie – marriage to a wealthy suitor – and in relation to her own position within the family.

One feature of Agnes's narrative is the sense she has of her own devalued condition. Unappreciated by her family she is, by virtue of both her status as employee and woman, equally disregarded by the Bloomfields. Although she alludes to the lack of respect they accord her, the achievement of a position in the house of the landed gentry causes her sensitivity to questions of 'place' to become more acute and perhaps betrays her own class bias. These developments are figured in the arrangements for conveying the Murray party to church:

> If some of my pupils chose to walk and take me with them, it was well for me; otherwise, my position in the carriage was to be crushed into the corner farthest from the open window, and with my back to the horses, a position which invariably made me sick; and, if I were not actually obliged to leave the church in the middle of the service, my devotions were disturbed with a feeling of languor and sickliness, and the tormenting fear of its becoming worse; and a depressing head-ache was generally my companion throughout the day, which would otherwise have been one of welcome rest, and holy, calm enjoyment. (*AG* 126–7)

As well as illustrating Agnes's marginalization within the family, this passage shows how her attempts at spiritual communion are overtaken by more bodily concerns. Her Christian fortitude becomes ever more compromised as she not only endures the insensitivities of her social superiors but has to negotiate their influence on the servants who are, properly speaking, Agnes's inferiors. Despite her attempts to protect these fellow employees 'against the tyranny and injustice of their young masters and mistresses' (*AG* 128), she does not gain their respect. Instead, their attitude towards Agnes is regulated by the example the Murrays set. Notwithstanding this test to her 'Christian humility', Agnes does eventually elicit 'symptoms of esteem' in Rosalie and Matilda. At this point, Agnes's growing self-consciousness is underlined by the way in which she imagines herself to be perceived by the girls:

> Miss Grey was a queer creature; she never flattered, and did not praise them half enough, but whenever she did speak favourably of them, or anything belonging to them, they could be quite sure her approbation was sincere....She had her own opinions on every subject, and kept steadily to them – very tiresome opinions they often were, as she was always thinking of what was right and what was wrong, and had a strange reverence for matters connected with religion, and an unaccountable liking to good people. (*AG* 129)

As Agnes here imagines herself receiving a qualified acceptance by the Murray family, she also becomes preoccupied by her own gendered status. The limited respect she appears to have earned as a governess does not compensate for losses she must also incur in the future – in the shapes of marriage and motherhood.

In 'The "Coming Out"' (chapter seven), Agnes draws attention to the transitional status of Rosalie who, now 18, '[is] to emerge from the quiet obscurity of the school-room into the full blaze of the fashionable world' (*AG* 130). This prospect seems to highlight the class differences which shape the respective futures of Agnes and Rosalie as well as their very different notions of what it means to be a woman. Whereas Agnes leaves behind one school-room for another in her attempt to prove her maturity, Rosalie's entrance into the 'fashionable world' is simply a prelude to marriage. The recent marriage of Agnes's own sister Mary 'To Mr Richardson, the vicar of a neighbouring parish' (*AG* 131), is revealed in this chapter which introduces the crucial romance that will dominate the remainder of the novel. Rosalie's excited account of the coming ball is coupled with her interrogation of Agnes over the content of Mary's letter. In the exchange between them Rosalie's priorities are shown to be wealth, looks and age, while Agnes values the moral standing of her sister's husband. At this point, the narrative prefigures the respective destinies of Rosalie and Agnes: although the one acquires a wealthy husband, she enters into a loveless marriage with a man she despises, while Agnes's less mercenary values ensure that she, like her sister, will live in relative comfort in a more loving relationship.

Rosalie's career as 'coquet with all the world' (*AG* 136) is witnessed by Agnes, who sees her exploitation of the men unlucky enough to fall under her spell and observes her wilful disregard for their feelings. The view Agnes has of Rosalie's dealings with her suitors is supplemented by the girl's own accounts which she relays to her governess/confidante. Although Rosalie's questioning of Agnes over Mary's letter indicates the criteria which inform her choice of husband, she comes to disregard her own prescriptions when she sets about the business of conquering her male suitors. One of these is Mr Hatfield, a clergyman whose vanity (as Agnes recognizes) is such that he cannot see that he is an unsuitable match.

However, it is not simply Hatfield's vanity which diminishes him in the eyes of the governess. She also pays attention to his performance as a figure of Christian authority. Agnes's perceptions of Rosalie and Hatfield underscore the extent to which both of them transgress gender boundaries. Rosalie uses her beauty in the pursuit of power over men and Hatfield supplements the power granted him as clergyman with a display which would not look out of place on a woman. As Agnes writes, he:

> would come sailing up the aisle, or rather sweeping along like a whirlwind, with his rich silk gown flying behind him and rustling against the pew doors, mount the pulpit like a conqueror ascending his triumphal car; then, sinking on the velvet cushion in an attitude of studied grace, remain in silent prostration for a certain time, then mutter over a Collect, and gabble through the Lord's prayer, rise, draw off one bright lavender glove to give the congregation the benefit of his sparkling rings, lightly pass his fingers through his well-curled hair, flourish a cambric handkerchief, recite a very short passage, or, perhaps, a mere phrase of Scripture, as a head-piece to his discourse, and, finally, deliver a composition, which as a composition, might be considered good, though far too studied and too artificial to be pleasing to me. (*AG* 140)

Hatfield's self-inflated pomposity stands in direct contrast to the new curate, Weston, who, though described by Rosalie as 'ugly', is defended by the more circumspect Agnes. Weston's introduction into the narrative once more pitches the different value systems of Rosalie and Agnes against each other. Whereas Rosalie attends to his appearance and lack of deference towards her, Agnes insists on reserving judgement: 'I cannot pretend to judge a man's character by a single, cursory glance at his face'. What Agnes claims to have noticed is Weston's 'style of reading' (*AG* 138), about which she is complimentary. Agnes's initial appreciation for Weston is redoubled when she hears him preach for, as she says, she is 'decidedly pleased with the evangelical truth of his doctrine, as well as the earnest simplicity of his manner, and the clearness and force of his style'. This apparently disinterested appreciation of the professional performance of the clergyman is later supplemented, and compromised, by an increasing interest in the more secular appeal of 'the beautiful Mr Weston' (*AG* 139).

Agnes's insistence, throughout her narrative, on connecting the abuse of power within the home to the interactions which take place outside it, is the focus of 'The Cottagers', the chapter in which she extends her observations on the performance of Rosalie and Matilda to include their behaviour towards the lower classes. Agnes's own limited success as their governess is suggested when she comments that 'chiefly owing to their defective education' the girls 'comported themselves towards their inferiors in a manner that was highly disagreeable'. Ostensibly fulfilling their duty towards the 'poor cottagers on their father's estate' (*AG* 143), the girls derive pleasure from the uneven exchanges which take place with 'an order of beings entirely distinct from themselves'. In return for minor acts of charity, Rosalie and Matilda believe 'the people must adore them as angels of light condescending to minister to their necessities, and enlighten their humble dwellings'. Agnes's attempts to correct the girls' misconceptions about the 'stupid and brutish' poor are tempered by her desire to achieve this end 'without alarming their pride, which was easily offended, and not soon appeased' (*AG* 144), for while Agnes enjoys a better standing than the cottagers, she too is dependent on the good opinion of her charges.

In her dealings with Nancy Brown, one of the cottagers, Agnes demonstrates her own version of Christian charity, as well as discovering more about the relative virtues of Hatfield and Weston. These two church representatives are measured against each other according to their responses to Nancy's spiritual and physical needs. In response to Nancy's spiritual crisis, Hatfield dictates a course which is as physically challenging to her as it is doctrinally rigid. Weston, on the other hand, provides for Nancy's physical well-being while also offering her advice which seems to validate Agnes's own spiritual values: 'if you cannot feel positive affection for those who do not care for you, you can at least try to do to them as you would they should do unto you' (*AG* 151–2). Nancy's revelation of the curate's behaviour towards her and the doctrine he espouses leaves Agnes 'feeling nearly as happy as herself' (*AG* 153), although she offers no explanation for this sudden elation. As her narrative progresses, however, it becomes clear that Agness initial appreciation of Weston's 'style' of ministering encompasses a more secular concern. The curate's preachings are as seductive as they are edifying to Agnes.

Agnes's characteristic spirituality takes on a different cast when Weston becomes the subject of her contemplations. Agnes legitimates her desire for Weston by recalling the deprivation she has thus far had to endure:

> In returning to the lodge, I felt very happy, and thanked God that I had now something to think about, something to dwell on as a relief from the weary monotony, the lonely drudgery of my present life – for I *was* lonely – never, from month to month, from year to year, except during my brief intervals of rest at home, did I see one creature to whom I could open my heart, or freely speak my thoughts with any hope of sympathy, or even comprehension. (*AG* 154)

This final admission of the cumulative effects of her social isolation enables Agnes to understand her 'exultation' (*AG* 154) as the product of many years of neglect. She goes as far as to compare her condition to that of 'one civilized man...doomed to pass a dozen years amid a race of intractable savages' and at risk of becoming 'a barbarian himself'.[13] As if to complete this wilderness-scenario, Weston's arrival is figured as the prospect of salvation and enlightenment:

> Already, I seemed to feel my intellect deteriorating, my heart petrifying, my soul contracting, and I trembled lest my very moral perceptions should become deadened, my distinctions of right and wrong confounded, and all my better faculties be sunk, at last, beneath the baleful influence of such a mode of life. The gross vapours of earth were gathering round me, and closing in upon my inward heaven; and thus it was that Mr Weston rose at length upon me, appearing like a morning star in my horizon, to save me from the fear of utter darkness; and I rejoiced that I had now a subject for contemplation that was above me, not beneath. (*AG* 155)

The sudden revelation of Agnes's imminent intellectual, moral and spiritual dissolution legitimates her new found interest in the male 'subject for contemplation' but does not entirely mask sexual desire. It does, however, suggest that Agnes is willing to submit to a hierarchy if it is based upon worth. The timely arrival of Weston on Agnes's forlorn 'horizon' leads her to contemplate the physical rather than spiritual attributes of her saviour. Her description of Weston and the admission that she likes 'to see' as well as 'hear' the curate, suggest the physical attraction Agnes experiences. This is mediated by an equal emphasis on the way in which his physical features confirm his moral character. The question of narrative propriety is raised when Agnes begins to discourse on Weston's smile before constraining herself on the grounds that such a commentary would involve chronological disruption: 'but I will not speak of that yet, for, at the time I mention, I had never seen him smile' (*AG* 156). If Agnes's sense of narrative order prevails here, her disciplined intercession nonetheless affirms that a more intimate relation between herself and Weston will be forthcoming. In this respect, although it is possible to read the concealment of desire as the reflex of Brontë's own sense of textual propriety, it is also likely that the hint of a coming intimacy between Agnes and Weston is designed to seduce the reader with prospects of romance.

Although Agnes's relation to Rosalie and their contrary value systems is the principal narrative focus during her time with the Murrays, the difference between Agnes and Rosalie is eventually eroded by Agnes's desire for Weston. As Matus notes, 'she obliquely confesses to the very emotions and desires that subvert the bland and dispassionate face of feminine respectability to which she lays claim'.[14] One example of this comes when both women anticipate the spectacle afforded by church attendance, though for Rosalie the pleasure relates to being seen rather than seeing. Given Agnes's apparent invisibility in the eyes of the other respectable church-goers, Weston's companionship on the homeward trek confirms, at last, her place in the limited village society. The courting couples, as Agnes notes 'talked over me or across, and if their eyes, in speaking, chanced to fall on me, it seemed as if they looked on vacancy – as if they either did not see me, or were very desirous to make it appear so' (*AG* 162). Weston, on the other hand, does notice Agnes and, in a quintessentially romantic gesture, offers to gather the flowers she dreams of from the grass bank. Agnes's characteristically guarded narrative admits her 'gratitude' to Weston but ascribes it to the fact that she is 'unaccustomed ... to receive such civilities' (*AG* 163). Her emphasis on Christian and moral duties begins to falter when she contemplates Weston's comments on his own lack of place. Although Weston's homeless state – his lack of familial attachments – calls forth both pity and 'sympathy' on the part of Agnes, it is offset by the opportunities afforded him as a man. Thus, Agnes muses, Weston's condition is better than her own because he has agency when it comes to the pursuit of the objects of his desire:

> 'he leads an active life; and a wide field for useful exertion lies before him, he can *make* friends – and he can make a home too, if he pleases, and doubtless he will please some time; and God grant the partner of that home may be worthy of his choice, and make it a happy one . . . such a home as he deserves to have! And how delightful it would be to –' But no matter what I thought. (*AG* 165-6)

Following this censored fantasy, Agnes admits to the reader that her original 'intention of concealing nothing' has been revised. Refusing to give voice to her own desire for a place in Weston's imaginary home, Agnes concludes the chapter by relating the teasing she endures concerning Weston from the perceptive Rosalie. Agnes's rejection of the 'appropriate fictions coined for the occasion' (*AG* 166) by Rosalie and Matilda with regard to her relation to Weston represents an equally self-conscious moment in the narrative. The stories the girls concoct relate to romantic intrigues but also might be said to call attention to the way in which Agnes has constructed her own narrative. As the instructional mode gives way to romance and the text registers an anxiety about the process of revealing female desire, the question of the appropriateness of Brontë's own fiction is highlighted. The anxiety is voiced by Agnes herself when she describes one of her meetings with Weston but omits 'to give a detail of his words, from a notion that they would not interest the reader . . . and not because I have forgotten them'. Notwithstanding her reservations about the propriety of her narrative, Agnes still attests to the power of her own recollection of Weston. She produces this 'confession' despite her fear that it looks 'absurd' and because she is assured of her own anonymity: 'they that read it will not know the writer' (*AG* 175).

As well as competing for Weston, both Agnes and Rosalie share in a desire to prove themselves to their mothers, Agnes through governessing and Rosalie through what she knows will be an eventual capitulation to her mother's wish that she marry Sir Thomas Ashby. If Rosalie is aware of the limited time available to her for the pursuit of more conquests, Agnes begins to measure herself against the more powerful allure of the younger, wealthier girl. Failing, on one occasion, to secure the attentions of Weston, she writes:

> It might be partly owing to my own stupidity, my want of tact and assurance; but I felt myself wronged; I trembled with apprehension; and I listened with envy to her easy, rapid flow of utterance, and saw with anxiety the bright smile with which she looked into his face from time to time, for she was walking a little in advance, for the purpose (as I judged) of being seen as well as heard. (*AG* 186)

As Agnes contemplates the relation between Rosalie and Weston, she not only measures herself against Rosalie but begins to doubt that Weston's judgement will withstand the attentions of the younger girl. When it appears as if Agnes's moral superiority is no match for Rosalie's charm and wealth, she is plunged into a crisis. Her characteristic rationalism fails and she succumbs to 'a passionate burst of tears' only curtailed by 'the odious bell for the school-room dinner' (*AG* 187). Called back to her duties, she must put aside her own feelings and bear witness to Rosalie's manipulations of Weston and her desire to make him feel her 'power' (*AG* 191). From her own disempowered position, Agnes not only struggles against envy for her rival but also her own conscience. Disavowing the sexual desire she experiences by claiming 'it is not the man, it is his goodness that I love', she nonetheless admits to the possible confusion of spiritual and sexual attraction, fearing that the former masks the latter:

> at church I might look without fear of scorn or censure upon a form and face more pleasing to me than the most beautiful of God's creations; I might listen without disturbance to a voice more charming than the sweetest music to my ears; I might seem to hold communion with that soul in which I felt so deeply interested, and imbibe its purest thoughts and holiest aspirations, with no alloy to such felicity, except the secret reproaches of my conscience, which would too often whisper that I was deceiving my own self, and mocking God with the service of a heart more bent upon the creature than the Creator. (*AG* 188)

As Agnes's narrative becomes dominated by romantic concerns, the movement from public interest to private drama is marked by a chapter entitled 'Confessions'. Her contemplation of

Weston's appearance is matched by pained self-reflection as Agnes weighs her own physical attributes and finds them wanting. Agnes's recognition of her own lack of beauty leads her to question the ground of her belief that 'If the mind be but well cultivated, and the heart well disposed, no one ever cares for the exterior'. This view, advanced by 'the teachers of our childhood' and passed on by Agnes herself, is queried by 'actual experience' (*AG* 192). The shift in perspective is underlined by Agnes's use of analogies drawn from nature, in which. she features as the 'humble-glow worm' destined to 'live and die alone' for want of the 'power to make her presence known' (*AG* 193). Agnes's willingness to draw on natural imagery at this point in order to illuminate her own dilemma extends to include Rosalie, characterized as a dog 'gorged to the throat' with her conquests, who will 'gloat over what [she] cannot devour, and grudge the smallest morsel to a starving brother' (*AG* 196). Once again, Agnes is mindful of the reader's view of her 'folly and weakness' (*AG* 200), as she struggles against her passion and strives to reconcile herself to the comforts of religion alone. These struggles are frequently undercut by Agnes's own prayers, in which she asks God to intercede on Weston's behalf to prevent his ensnarement by Rosalie and, by implication, to secure him for herself.

On the marriage of Rosalie to Ashby, Agnes's remaining charge, Matilda, becomes the renewed focus of the family's attention. Matilda's continued refusal to maintain the decorum which befits her becomes a more pressing problem since she is now to be groomed for marriage, and it leads her father to comment that she is 'not quite what a young lady ought to be'. The question of Agnes's responsibility as a governess, together with her influence, is again foregrounded and becomes the subject of Mrs Murray's criticism. The task of amusing Matilda, now forbidden to wander through the 'yards, stables, kennels, and coach-house' (*AG* 205), falls to Agnes, who must find ways of guiding the girl towards more feminine pursuits. Mrs Murray insists that the status of Matilda is inextricably linked to that of her governess. Agnes's own 'merits' will be judged according to 'the young ladies she professes to have educated'. Matilda's apparent lack of 'taste' (*AG* 206) and her failure to conform to a feminine ideal is blamed on the governess, but this narrative return to the question of education is only temporary, for Agnes's own interests clearly lie elsewhere.

With the death of her father, Agnes's career as a private governess is brought to an end. However, while the romantic plot of the novel appears to be moving towards conventional closure – the marriage of Agnes and Weston – this event is delayed. Not only does Weston disappear from sight but the course of Agnes's life after the death of her father also demonstrates her emotional and financial independence. Mrs Grey's refusal to return to her wealthy family as errant but reformed daughter indicates her continued commitment to the principles upon which she had based her marriage. As Meyer argues, this subverts the conventions of the nineteenth-century novel since it 'evokes the possibility...of such a restoration of originary class status and has the protagonists reject it'.[15] Yet while Mrs Grey remains loyal to her husband's memory, Agnes struggles with her own passion for Weston and the illness it brings on. While Agnes perceives this struggle as a refusal to allow 'mere inventions of the imagination' to govern her emotional state, it also represents a period of mourning, less for her father than a love lost:

> at last, I gave up hoping, for even my heart acknowledged it was all in vain. But still, I would think of him; I would cherish his image in my mind; and treasure every word, look, and gesture that my memory could retain; and brood over his excellences, and his peculiarities, and, in fact, all I had seen, heard, or imagined respecting him. (*AG* 224)

Once Agnes successfully controls both memory and imagination her health returns and she rechannels her energies into 'the work that God' (*AG* 225) sets before her in the form of running the school she has established with her mother. Their means of achieving economic independence is directly contrasted to that of Rosalie, now installed as 'a prisoner and a slave' (*AG* 237) at Ashby Park and refusing to attend to her new daughter on the grounds that the child will eventually 'eclipse' her and 'enjoy those pleasures' (*AG* 238) she is denied. Rosalie's fate vindicates Agnes's disapproving stance towards the flirtatious girl who once claimed that 'reformed rakes make the best husbands' (*AG* 172). Rosalie's regret and her desire for Agnes's friendship suggest her own reform, as does her hope that Agnes will be her daughter's governess so that her child will be brought 'up in the way it should go' and become 'a better woman...than its mamma' (*AG* 226). Yet while Rosalie wishes Agnes to become both friend and governess-in-waiting, the social constraints placed upon her ensure that the possibility of friendship will always be limited. Agnes can visit and advise her former charge but cannot properly be included within the society at Ashby Park.

Agnes's narrative closes with the return of Weston and the offer of his hand in marriage. Her brief account of their life together glosses 'his faults' as a man and emphasizes his achievement as 'a pastor, a husband [and] a father' (*AG* 251), appearing to confirm Meyer's insight that 'Agnes's marriage has a silencing effect'.[16] Announcing her joint role as mother and teacher as well as the financial security she and her husband have attained through their economy, Agnes suggests that, unlike the other women who feature in the narrative, she is able to fulfil her obligations to her children. Though Agnes is in some sense silenced at the end of the novel, the description of her married life returns the narrative to the understated failings of a father who jeopardizes his family's future through his speculations and a mother who neglects to prepare her daughter for the demands of an independent life as either governess or wife. As such, the social critique offered by *Agnes Grey* extends to include her own family as much as her employers. The novel also suggests that Agnes finally secures the independence she has sought by 'revers[ing] the order of things' in the establishment of a different set of values.

2

Spatial Politics in
The Tenant of Wildfell Hall

> She who undertakes the cleansing of a careless bachelor's apartment
> will be liable to more abuse for the dust she raises, than
> commendation for the clearance she effects.[1]

The publication of *The Tenant of Wildfell Hall* (1848) drew such
opprobrium from Anne Brontë's critics that she felt compelled,
in the preface to the second edition, to write a belated defence of
the novel. She begins with a modest acknowledgement of 'the
praises' the novel 'has elicited from a few kind critics', before
turning to more negative responses. These Brontë describes as
'more bitter than just' (*TWH* 3), rebutting them in the remainder
of her preface by emphasizing the moral and religious
imperatives which govern her writing.

Echoing the sentiments of her fictional ally, Agnes Grey,
Brontë first expresses the hope that her narrative will 'amuse' as
well as 'benefit' her readers but goes on to revise the apparent
endorsement of such balanced objectives. More defiant than
Agnes, she announces a willingness to sacrifice her own
reputation and, if necessary, the 'reader's immediate pleasure'
in order to fulfil her 'duty to speak an unpalatable truth, with
the help of God' (*TWH* 5).

The subject of Brontë's epistolary novel is the life of Mrs
Graham, a woman of unknown origin who, accompanied by her
young son, takes up the tenancy at Wildfell Hall. Pursued by
Gilbert Markham, the son of a neighbouring farmer, Mrs
Graham reveals the history which drove her to seek refuge at
Wildfell Hall. She does so by allowing Gilbert to read her
journal. It reveals her real identity as Helen Huntington, the

estranged and fugitive wife of the aristocratic, alcoholic and debauched Arthur Huntington. The journal details Helen's years of mistreatment by her wayward husband along with her escape to the relative isolation of Wildfell Hall where she supports herself and her son through her artwork. Following the revelation of Helen's history she hears her husband has been injured in a riding accident and returns, dutifully, to nurse him through his final days. His death eventually frees Helen to marry Gilbert.

An overview of contemporary responses to *The Tenant* suggests that it is not only the text which receives harsh critical judgement but also the author herself. A characteristic response comes from one anonymous critic who identifies in Brontë 'a morbid love for the coarse, not to say the brutal'.[2] Another critic warns Anne (and Emily indeed) 'against their fancy for dwelling upon what is disagreeable',[3] a position upheld by a further reader who identifies the metaphorical signatures of both writers by 'the prominence given to the brutal element of human nature'[4] in their novels. The 'opinion' of *Sharpe's London Magazine* is perhaps the most vehement in its condemnation of *The Tenant*:

> so revolting are many of the scenes, so coarse and disgusting the language put into the mouths of some of the characters, that the reviewer to whom we entrusted it returned it to us, saying it was unfit to be noticed in the pages of *Sharpe*; and we are so far of the same opinion, that our object in the present paper is to warn our readers, and more especially our lady-readers, against being induced to peruse it.[5]

The 'reviewer' in question pinpoints as a specific source of offence 'the disgustingly truthful minuteness' with which Brontë writes in 'the scenes which occur after the drinking bouts'. These scenes alone provide, in his opinion, definitive 'proof of the unreadableness'[6] of Brontë's novel. The explicit nature of *The Tenant* is also noted by a critic in the *Rambler* who, using a similar idiom, draws attention to how the novel 'detail[s] with offensive minuteness … disgusting scenes of debauchery, blasphemy and profaneness'.[7] A more positive view of the novel is offered by Charles Kingsley, who objects to the 'unnecessary coarseness' of the text, but does so on the grounds that it 'injures the real usefulness and real worth of the book'.[8] Yet, like *Sharpe's London Magazine*, Kingsley still claims that the novel is 'utterly unfit to be put into the hands of girls',[9] while also wishing that 'every man in England might read and lay to heart [the] horrible record'[10] provided by Helen Graham's diary. Kingsley's desire to protect female readers from the text and the men it represents contrasts starkly with Brontë's own stance. Although doubting her competence 'to reform the errors and abuses of society', she nonetheless defines as vital the more individual use to which the novel might be put by would-be Huntingtons and Helens: 'if I have warned one rash youth from following in [Huntington's] steps, or prevented one thoughtless girl from falling into the very natural error of my heroine, the book has not been written in vain' (*TWH* 4).

Responses to *The Tenant* such as these indicate that the 'unpalatable truth' to which Brontë refers in her preface relates to the detailed account of aristocratic debauchery which dominates the novel. Yet since it is conveyed primarily through Helen's diary, this 'truth' can be said to reside in a woman's disturbing experiences of courtship, marriage and motherhood. As a female *bildungsroman*, the novel not only shows how Helen negotiates male power and corruption, but also demonstrates the extent to which the private lives of married couples are informed by the social structures in which they are enmeshed and the ideological forces which operate upon them. Nowhere is this more apparent than in Helen's diary, which ostensibly deals with romantic, domestic and familial relations but becomes the vehicle for a wider social, political and cultural critique.

In contrast to the terms of this summary of *The Tenant*, Terry Eagleton identifies a weakness in the novel which he relates to its continual foregrounding of 'personal suffering and self-fulfilment' within the framework of a 'traditional love-story'. Such a weakness, he argues, ensures that the novel effectively 'dissolves the social to the individual' and enables Brontë to bypass wider conflicts. At the same time as emphasizing the text's political evasiveness, Eagleton highlights its 'relative separation of the personal and social',[11] a feature of the text which he illustrates by considering the characters within it. Collecting them into two distinct groups, he suggests that they present the reader with equally unconvincing extremes. Under the first grouping Eagleton places 'aristocratic villains', 'mechanically reducible to their social determinants'. Nominated for the second group are the chief protagonists, described by Eagleton as 'too abstractly individuated, too internally unpressured by the strains and frictions of their social world'.[12] The granting of credence to these groupings suggests that Brontë acknowledges the influence of social and cultural forces selectively rather than that she fails to engage with them at all. Eagleton's analysis seems to break down because of the contrary movements he identifies in the text. The dissolution of 'the social to the individual' would seem to be incomplete for, as Eagleton's analysis of the characters suggests, some individuals do embody the social determinants which ought to have been subsumed by the romance conventions operating on the novel.

Eagleton's reading fails at precisely the point he tries to substantiate the claim that the text retreats into the individual concerns of the bourgeois subject. His own failure to clarify the distinction between the ego-centred and socially engaged dimensions of a text is unsurprising for, as recent theories of subjectivity suggest, 'identity' is 'precariously constituted in the discourses of the social whereby it is both determined and regulated by the forces of power inherent in a given social formation, but capable also of undermining them'.[13] Aside from theoretical objections to Eagleton's reading, his analysis of *The Tenant* assumes that its romantic concerns not only dominate the narrative but also compromise its potential for social and political engagement. He sets up an opposition between the individual/personal realm and the external world which is not only questionable but, in relation to *The Tenant*, also ironic. Brontë's novel not only demonstrates that the individual is subject to powerful ideological forces which delineate his or her place within culture and society, but that there are ways in which these forces can be subverted and resisted by those who suffer as a result. In a narrative which dramatizes the complex interplay between subject and society by focusing on the marital experience of a woman, Brontë highlights the extent to which the internal and supposedly private realms of desire and domesticity are also intensely political. In its insistence that 'the personal is political' the text resonates with the feminist slogan which informed the theorizing of gender relations in the 1960s while, at the same time, breaking through the silence which surrounded the institution of marriage in the early to mid

Victorian era. At its most radical the novel makes visible the private realm, revealing those forces which structure desire and domesticity to a very public and critical scrutiny. In this respect, Eagleton's belittling of the romantic and 'personal' concerns of the narrative, and his insistence that these obscure the 'social' realm which ought to be the subject of fiction, represents a crucial oversight on the part of the Marxist critic. As feminist readings of Victorian literature and culture have shown, such an opposition between the private and public underpins the ideology of 'separate spheres' and the institution of marriage itself.[14] This private/public dichotomy is dismantled by *The Tenant*, not only through the intimate revelations which are the subject of Helen's diary and constitute a powerful critique of masculinity and patriarchal power, but also by means of a sophisticated exploration of various forms of space – textual, social and bodily.

TEXTUAL SPACE

The Tenant begins and ends with Gilbert Markham's letter to his friend Jack Halford, in which he sets out to heal the breach which has occurred between them. The cause of this rift is Gilbert's failure to reciprocate Halford's 'very particular and interesting account of the most remarkable occurrences of [his] early life' with some 'story-telling' of his own. Writing to his friend, whom he acknowledges as a 'deeply injured man', Gilbert sets out 'to atone' (*TWH* 9) for his previous wrongdoing with a tale which will complete the confidential exchange between them.

The Tenant has been described as 'the longest single-narrative, enclosing epistolary novel of the nineteenth-century'.[15] Gilbert's preamble to chapter one establishes the epistolary framework of the novel but does so in a way which highlights the significance of 'story-telling' as a medium through which intimacy between men can be secured. In reciprocating Halford's gesture of friendship, Gilbert allays accusations of 'ingratitude and unfriendly reserve', offering his own autobiography as a means of overcoming division. The relationship between the two men is not simply grounded in their friendship though, because it later emerges that Halford is married to Gilbert's sister, Rose. The exchange thus also takes place within a familial context. It is rendered even more complex, however, because Gilbert's narrative focuses on his relationship with the woman – Helen – who becomes his wife. In order to produce a 'full and faithful account' of the events he wishes to describe, he draws upon 'certain musty old letters' along with a 'faded old journal' of his own. The inclusion of the former is clearly signalled in the narrative which follows, while the contents of the latter are absorbed into Gilbert's retrospective account of the 'circumstances connected with the most important event of [his] life'. The major part of his narrative takes the form, however, of an account drawn from Helen's diary, of her previous marriage. Its centrality suggests that Gilbert is actually offering her story, rather than his own, in exchange for Halford's. This passing of a woman's story between men in order to repair their intimacy represents an act of appropriation. Gilbert appears to be in possession of his wife's diary, which he not only transcribes but also edits. In passing on the text to Halford, albeit in modified form, Gilbert repeats a gesture made by his wife when, at a crucial point in their relationship, she loans her diary to him so that he might know her history. If Helen's act helps facilitate sexual intimacy, its repetition by Gilbert promotes homosocial bonding. This point is underscored by Gilbert when he acknowledges that his introduction to Helen constitutes 'the most important event' of his life, but also qualifies this statement by adding, 'previous to [his] acquaintance with Jack Halford at least' (*TWH* 10). The importance of the homosocial in Gilbert's narrative is further illustrated in his relationship with Helen's brother, Mr Lawrence. Their friendship is forged by Lawrence's proximity to the object of Gilbert's desire, as Gilbert admits when he comments that he 'never sought his company but with the hope of hearing something about her' (*TWH* 438). It develops into a more intimate relationship once Lawrence begins to allow Gilbert to read for himself the letters Helen sends. Submitted to Gilbert's 'longing gaze' (*TWH* 432) or alternatively 'devoured' with his eyes, these letters are memorized and their contents, or at least 'the most important passages' (*TWH* 439), entered into his own journal.

Although Gilbert adheres to Helen's instruction that he

should return her diary once it is read, it seems as if his acquisition of the text, or at least his access to it, becomes permanent once the two are married. Offering 'an abbreviation of [the diary's] contents' to Halford, Gilbert also repeats the gesture of censorship made by Helen when she passes the text to him after 'hastily' tearing 'a few leaves from the end'. These last pages refer to Helen's perceptions of Gilbert, whose arrival in the diary brings about its abrupt closure. Gilbert justifies his editorial activities on grounds of relevance but also in aesthetic terms: he claims to remove only 'a few passages here and there of merely temporal interest to the writer, or such as would serve to encumber the story rather than elucidate it' (*TWH* 129). In the interests of improving the narrative, Gilbert not only removes portions of the text but also, it seems, adds chapter headings to it.

Gilbert's use of his wife's diary and letters clearly foregrounds the extent to which the circulation of particular texts facilitates social exchange, as well as raising more contentious issues relating to the dissemination of a private narrative and simultaneous appropriation of a female text. For Gilbert and Helen the diary also has a valuable social function, protecting, as it does, their respective reputations: it works to defend the one from the accusations of Halford and the other from scurrilous gossip concerning her sexual *mores*. It is less apparent whether the particular use to which Gilbert puts his wife's diary is known to her. He writes for Halford's amusement while enjoying the privacy of his 'library' when 'the family are absent on a visit' (*TWH* 10), and does not acknowledge the presence of his wife until the close of his letter. Helen's attitude towards such a transaction between friends might well be adduced from the comments she makes on the nature of epistolary communication, to which she must resort when separated from Huntington during the early stages of their marriage. In his absence she must content herself with the letters he promises to write, longing for a reunion when they can enjoy an 'exchange [of] thoughts without the intervention of these cold go-betweens, pen, ink, and paper' (*TWH* 200). Once Helen begins to doubt the sincerity of Huntington's writings and promises, she also questions the status of her own communiqués, wondering whether they are displayed by Huntington to his friends.

The complex exchange and interchange of texts in the novel is one aspect of its narrative structure which has attracted much critical attention. While contemporary reviewers voice objections to the novel's subject matter, they also express reservations concerning its form. As one anonymous critic writes:

> To say the truth, there is no very intense excitement in any part of the book. Just at the time when we begin to feel some interest about Markham and the lady, we are thrown back upon her previous history, which occupies a full half of the three volumes before us. This is a fatal error: for, after so long and minute a history, we cannot go back and recover the enthusiasm which we have been obliged to dismiss a volume and a half before.[16]

More recent critics take a less dismissive view, addressing the use of letter, diary and journal, as well as the ordering of events within the narrative, as aspects of the novel that have an ideological as well as aesthetic function. For Lori A. Paige the diary performs a double function. Its first function relates to the manner of its composition and the fact that 'no entry occurs more than two days after the event described'. This lends authority to Helen's story, exempting it from 'critical disbelief or accusations of exaggeration'. The diary's second function relates to the way in which it draws attention to 'the larger context of the written word's role in the novel.'[17] Once it is passed to Gilbert, the diary works to facilitate his reform and therefore, like the novel itself, fulfils a didactic purpose. This doubling of diary and novel creates an alliance between Brontë and Helen since both proclaim a desire to reveal the truth. Paige's emphasis on the legitimizing effects of the diary is shared by Jan B. Gordon, even as Gordon's concern is less with the written than the spoken word. For Gordon, the diary acts as a corrective to the gossip, speculation and innuendo which circulate in the text and are the dominant form of communication in Helen's society. The diary counters these verbal distortions by rendering Helen's 'history...eligible for...a narrative consumption, in order that the private history which had been such a threat to community stability might become part of the community's collective fiction'. For Gordon, the diary effects the rehabilitation of Helen rather than the reform of Gilbert and becomes 'surely part of the socialization of Helen Huntington'[18] and, ultimately, enables her to be claimed for the purposes of remarriage. Elizabeth Langland also focuses on 'narrative exchange'[19] in the novel but reaches a less conservative conclusion than Gordon. She argues that the structure and form of *The Tenant* reflect the hierarchies which exist between men and women within society at large: 'by initially making Helen Graham an object of Gilbert's narrative and not the subject of her own, the text enacts what it also presents thematically: women's objectification and marginalization within patriarchal culture'.[20] This point is borne out by Laura C. Berry, who relates the narrative structure to changes concerning the legal status of women and children as property. '[I]n the end', she writes, 'Gilbert Markham...gets custody not only of little Arthur, but of the story of both Arthurs, of Helen, indeed of all the narrative'.[21]

Apart from its structural, social and ideological value, the diary has a private function to perform in relation to Helen, which changes throughout the course of its composition. Recording Helen's social debut, it begins by articulating a discontent with the suitors who approach her. It allows her to voice frustrations she must otherwise check and, increasingly, the desire she feels – for Huntington – which must equally remain hidden. Resonating with the emotional effects of her amatory encounters, the diary acts as 'a confidential friend into whose ear [she] might pour forth the overflowings of [her] heart' (*TWH* 154). As Helen's marital experiences become more extreme, it allows her to filter and reflect upon their more overwhelming aspects. She eventually relies upon it to state 'the case for [her] own satisfaction' (*TWH* 339) when she resolves to leave Huntington.

If the process of inscribing a blank space – be it paper or canvas – can be cathartic or liberating, it is also, as *The Tenant* demonstrates, a precarious undertaking for a woman. The text can be appropriated by another, reveal too much, or be misread. All of these possibilities are explored within the novel. The dangers of female self-inscription are dramatically rendered when Huntington discovers Helen's diary and reads in it her plans for escape. Her husband's brief glance at the text leads him to thwart these plans by confiscating all of her property and destroying her painting equipment – the means by which she hopes to earn her living once free from him. On learning Helen's escape-plan, Huntington revels in her apparent inability to 'keep [her] own secret', a failing he extrapolates out to all women and which works to his advantage: 'It's well these women must be blabbing – if they haven't a friend to talk to, they must whisper their secrets to the fishes, or write them on the sand or something'. Huntington's effusive 'self-congratulations' ironically give his wife the opportunity to 'secure [her] manuscript', thus preventing the additional 'humiliation of seeing it in his hands again' (*TWH* 367). The value of the text in the power-struggle between husband and wife clearly extends beyond the information it reveals at this point. Commenting that it is 'rather long' (*TWH* 364) as he temporarily casts it aside, Huntington does not realize its value as a repository for Helen's 'secret thoughts and recollections' and that she 'would sooner burn it all than he should read what [she] had written when [she was] such a fool as to love him!' The traces of Helen's former affections are clearly seen by her to constitute a potential source of ammunition for Huntington. Her desire to protect the book from her husband not only leads her to conceal it but also extends to include the process of editing out his words of abuse which, she asserts, she 'will not defile this paper with repeating' (*TWH* 367). Helen's protective stance towards the book underlines her perception of the text as a sacred but also vulnerable space, as she understands that the confidences it contains can lead to an unwanted exposure of female subjectivity. When she later tears away the pages which relate to Gilbert before allowing him to see the diary's contents, it is because she has learnt through experience the dangers to which her inscriptions leave her open. The diary not only records history but also has a history of its own. That it is later transcribed by Gilbert for Halford in order to revive their flagging intimacy suggests that its contents remain a potential source of unwarranted revelation for Helen.

The Tenant explores textual space by raising questions relating not only to the written word but also to other forms of inscription. In her second encounter with Huntington it is the 'daubs and scratches' of Milicent Hargrave which give him the opportunity to approach Helen under the pretext of joining in her critical scrutiny of the drawings. Yet this cover is barely maintained for, 'receiving the drawings, one by one from [Helen's] hand', he 'successively scanned them over, and threw them on the table, but said not a word about them, though he was talking all the time'. Helen's own disregard for the works and the artist is apparent when she comments, 'I don't know what Milicent Hargrave thought of such conduct, but *I* found his conversation extremely interesting' (*TWH* 144). The lapse of attention here cannot be solely explained by the content of Huntington's discourse which, Helen states, would not: 'appear anything very particular, if written here, without the adventitious aids of look, and tone, and gesture, and that ineffable but indefinite charm, which cast a halo over all he did and said, and would have made it a delight to look in his face, and hear the music of his voice, if he had been talking positive nonsense' (*TWH* 145). Although Helen's attraction to Huntington cannot be attributed to his intrinsic worth it is, despite Helen's reservations about written language, nonetheless transcribed in her diary. The subjective perception of the newly enamoured woman is recorded in her very attempt to explain his mysterious appeal. She focuses on the physical form of her lover in a way which suggests that her perception is motivated by passion. This point is confirmed by Helen's 'vexation' and 'strange...conduct' following her aunt's successful disruption of the encounter between Helen and Huntington, 'coming composedly forward, under pretence of wishing to see the drawings, that she cared and knew nothing about' (*TWH* 145). While both Huntington and Helen's aunt exploit the social conventions associated with the display of artworks, Helen also colludes with this strategy and – by implication – effects the erasure of another woman, the female artist, Milicent.

Helen's own desire to put her artistic skills to practical use suggests that female self-expression not only has a cathartic effect but also represents a source of economic liberation. However, like the diary, Helen's pictures can reveal too much to those who look closely enough and make her vulnerable to the male gaze. In the chapter entitled 'The Miniature', Helen is forced to negotiate this difficulty. In the first of two scenes, she exhibits her drawings to the assembled company but is horrified when Huntington turns his attention to the '*back* of the picture' she has offered for public scrutiny. His delight upon discovering 'his own face that [she] had sketched there and forgotten to rub out' leads him to pocket the evidence of her desire. Greedily gathering 'all the drawings to himself' (*TWH* 155), Huntington declares his intention to 'look at *both* sides now' and goes on to examine the remaining pieces. Helen's confidence that 'his vanity would not be gratified by any further discoveries' is short-lived:

> though I must plead guilty to having disfigured the backs of several with abortive attempts to delineate that too fascinating physiognomy, I was sure that, with that one unfortunate exception, I had carefully obliterated all such witnesses of my infatuation. But the pencil frequently leaves an impression upon cardboard that no amount of rubbing can efface. Such, it seems, was the case with most of these; and I confess I trembled when I saw him holding them so close to the candle, and poring so intently over the seeming blanks; but still, I trusted he would not be able to make out these dim traces to his own satisfaction. I was mistaken however – having ended his scrutiny, he quietly remarked, –
>
> 'I perceive, the backs of young ladies' drawings, like the postscripts of their letters, are the most important and interesting part of the concern.' (*TWH* 156)

Huntington looks behind the signs laid out for official display in order to uncover the traces of female desire. Helen's own language suggests that she understands her interest in Huntington to transgress conventional artistic and social codes. She sees her own portraits of Huntington to have 'disfigured' the card on which they feature while the faces themselves bear witness to her 'infatuation'. Since the aesthetic space available to Helen has been deployed in the name of sexual desires rather than to satisfy a demand for the display of feminine accomplishments, it appears that Huntington's actions entail a transgression of the boundary which separates the public from the private. His appropriation of the offending material does not curb Helen's sense of exposure though, since it comes to signify his possession of a text which stands as 'an eternal monument to his pride and [her] humiliation' (*TWH* 157).

In a subsequent scene, Huntington repeats his gesture of appropriation, when he discovers Helen's 'unfinished sketches'. Removing the 'bowels' from her portfolio, he filches 'a complete miniature portrait' (*TWH* 161) of himself. Helen's vehement protestations lead him to return the portrait, which she tears in two and deposits in the fire. This act of resistance satisfies Helen and vexes Huntington but also drives him to turn his attentions to Annabella Wilmot in order to punish a woman who has dared to thwart him.

In each of these scenes various forms of appropriation of a female aesthetic space are enacted. In the first, the conventions of display are used by Huntington and Helen's aunt alike in order to advance their own designs. In the other two scenes it is Helen's surreptitious use of artistic space which threatens to expose her desires for Huntington, filling in the 'blanks' with 'traces' which ought to be concealed. Later, when Helen's art becomes a source of economic independence, she is careful to disguise its origin. She signs her pictures with false initials and avoids depicting local landmarks, thereby obscuring both identity and place from potential viewers. Her portrait of Huntington is retained in order to compare his features to those of their son, but its face is turned to the wall. The distinctions between public and private space are repeatedly shown to be unstable, as the public is appropriated for private ends and the private is exposed to unwanted scrutiny.

SOCIAL SPACE

One of the ways in which *The Tenant* underlines the interconnectedness of subject and society is, paradoxically, through an emphasis on the many different boundaries which are established within society. These boundaries demarcate the ways in which the subject is constructed by the dominant ideology even as they are constantly transgressed – most obviously through Helen's efforts to liberate herself from patriarchal tyranny. The novel's concern with the politics of space is signalled not only through a complex narrative structure but also through an emphasis on place and placeless-ness. Helen's enigmatic position within her own family and apparent estrangement from her father suggest, from the outset, a displacement from origins.[22] While she asserts a familial independence by marrying Huntington, her romantic idealism leads to a state of imprisonment, presaged even on her 'bridal tour', where her desire to experience 'the continental scenes' displeases an egocentric husband unwilling for his wife to 'take delight in anything disconnected with himself'. Her first excursion into the wider world is curtailed, not only by Huntington's selfishness, but also by his history:

> He wanted to get me home, he said, to have me all to himself, and to see me safely installed as the mistress of Grassdale Manor…as if I had been some frail butterfly, he expressed himself fearful of rubbing the silver off my wings by bringing me into contact with society, especially that of Paris or Rome; and, moreover, he did not scruple to tell me that there were ladies in both places that would tear his eyes out if they happened to meet him with me. (*TWH* 203)

If Helen's first experience of marriage literally diminishes her horizons, she nonetheless persists in her belief that she will assume a position of power within the domestic realm. She hopes to exert a moral and spiritual influence over her retrograde partner and, especially, to counteract the influences which, she claims, have led him astray. Significantly, her desire to establish an ideal domestic haven at Grassdale is undermined by Huntington's insistence on bringing his sexual past – in the form of 'the whole story of his intrigue' (*TWH* 209) with a married woman – into this domestic sphere. The cause of their first quarrel, Huntington's account of this affair, leads Helen to regret the marriage and to lock him out of her bedroom chamber. As she removes herself from the sexually corrupt Huntington, Helen's gesture of exclusion and separation represents an attempt to re-establish boundaries between pure and impure spaces. Helen's defiance and her attempt to punish her husband's transgression set in motion a further division between the couple as Huntington similarly withdraws his company, choosing to spend lengthier periods away from home and thus establishes a pattern for the remainder of their marriage. During the course of the marriage Helen is only allowed one brief interlude in the capital city because of Huntington's fear she might become 'Londonized' by 'too much intercourse with the ladies of the world'. Both Huntington and Helen draw upon a gendered discourse in order to justify their respective occupation of town and country. Claiming 'no particular wish to mingle with the world', Helen retreats into the 'very domestic habits' (*TWH* 216) which are, as a woman, her entitlement. Huntington, for his part, relies on spurious business dealings to legitimate his absences. Yet the disposition and delineation of male and female space in this manner is not sustained in the remainder of the narrative, since Huntington's sojourns at home are rendered tolerable to him only by visits from his 'bachelor friends' (*TWH* 176). These men bring to Grassdale the vices in which they indulge when resident at the cosmopolitan 'club' which, in Huntington's view, serves as their exclusive and collective 'home' (*TWH* 188). These guests turn Helen's domestic retreat into an increasingly volatile realm, further eroding her influence over Huntington and overturning the conventions which govern respectable domesticity. Invading the domestic space, these men extend their corrupting influence to include Helen's son, demonstrating as such a contempt for female and maternal authority alike. However, if Helen's confrontation with a collective masculinity compromises her status as wife and mother, it is invasions by other women which ironically precipitate her final flight.

One of these women is Annabella, whose affair with Huntington prompts Helen's first attempt at escape. With the subsequent arrival of Huntington's mistress (the fake governess Miss Myers), Helen seeks 'to watch and scrutinize' (*TWH* 383) the behaviour of the couple. Her suspicions confirmed by the 'intelligence' (*TWH* 384) offered by her loyal servant Rachel, Helen resolves to flee immediately. As she prepares for escape, clandestinely gathering belongings together, Helen admits that she does 'not understand the art of stowing them into the boxes, so as to take up the smallest possible space' (*TWH* 386–7). She does, however, develop a strategy for dealing with the sexual threat posed by the illicit coupling of master and bogus governess. The transgression of class and convention which this affair represents is seen to endanger Helen's son more than herself. As she writes, 'I have laid him in my bed for better security, and never more, I trust, shall his innocent lips be defiled by their contaminating kisses, or his young ears polluted by their words' (*TWH* 387). In defence of her son, she retreats with him to her bedchamber as the text again figures the struggle for power in spatial terms. By the time she leaves Grassdale, Helen has endured the constant incursions of outsiders, which culminate in the arrival of a woman who, in her dual capacity as governess and mistress, comes to usurp her place as mother and wife and brings about her departure to Wildfell Hall.

Helen's enforced exile at Wildfell arouses the suspicions of the villagers who, confronted with the arrival of a single woman with a child, make every attempt to 'place' them within the social order. For her part, Helen avoids social interaction, not only to evade discovery but also to re-establish her own integrity, along with that of her son. She describes her new home as an 'asylum' (*TWH* 55), a term which at once signifies sanctuary and madhouse and comes to epitomize the novel's concern with the way in which, as Berry puts it, 'the guardianship of home can easily collapse into imprisonment'.[23]

Yet far from constituting a safe haven for Helen, Wildfell is, like Grassdale, breached by outsiders. The first and most important of these intruders is Gilbert who, despite his initial declaration, 'I would rather admire you from this distance, fair lady, than be the partner of your home' (*TWH* 17), is drawn to the gothic mansion and its enclosures where Helen is resident. His approach is tentative – 'I did not like to go quite to the front and stare in at the gate; but I paused beside the garden wall, and looked' (*TWH* 23) – but also fortuitous, since he saves Helen's son from tumbling off the wall. Gilbert's next incursion, in the company of 'Eliza Millward, Fergus and Rose' (*TWH* 59), is more direct since it takes the form of a social visit which nonetheless has a hidden purpose. This is voiced by Fergus who, with a typical lack of constraint, reveals that the collective show of neighbourliness is designed to satisfy a curiosity regarding Helen. Although Gilbert presents himself as a disinterested visitor more inclined to sit with Arthur while 'the young ladies baited his mother with small talk' (*TWH* 60), he proves less reserved when, on a subsequent trip to the sea, he overlooks Helen's artistic labours. His later encroachments into Helen's territory are as calculated as his dealings with the woman herself. Learning by experience what displeases, he avoids 'the sentimental or the complimentary' and limits his conversation to 'abstract matters, or topics of common interest' (*TWH* 72). While he confines his discussion to 'painting, poetry, and music, theology, geology and philosophy', Gilbert also advances it by loaning Helen books. This movement from conversational to material exchange reflects the overall strategy Gilbert adopts in order to breach Helen's threshold. He proves to be particularly astute when he realizes he can exploit Helen's maternal affections and is not above using Arthur in order to ingratiate himself:

> My first pretext for invading the sanctum was to bring Arthur a little waddling puppy...which delighted the child beyond expression, and, consequently, could not fail to please his mamma. My second was to bring him a book, which, knowing his mother's particularity, I had carefully selected, and which I had submitted for her approbation before presenting it to him. Then, I brought her some plants for the garden, in my sister's name – having previously persuaded Rose to send them. Each of these times I enquired after the picture she was painting from the sketch taken on the cliff, and was admitted into the studio, and asked my opinion or advice respecting its progress. (*TWH* 73)

While Gilbert marks his progress with Helen in terms of his access to her 'hermitage' (*TWH* 73), the conflation of person and place which the use of this word implies is also less generously prefigured by his mother. On receiving the news of the arrival of 'a single lady' at Wildfell, she exclaims: 'Good gracious, my dear! The place is in ruins!' (*TWH* 14), linking the disrepair of Helen's new abode to its occupant's dubious history. The attempts of the respectable community to uncover this history with polite and, in the case of Fergus, less than polite questioning, fail to satisfy a collective need to position her by reading her past. Helen's reticence gives rise to endless gossip and even her stance on child-rearing calls forth objections from the women and interference from the Vicar, who feels a moral, public and professional obligation to guide her in domestic affairs. The powerful maternal forces which Gilbert exploits in his relation to Helen are subject to critical scrutiny by the entire community, whose comments and interventions, masquerading as concern, represent a metaphorical form of trespass.

The breaking down of the distinction between public and private space which this represents is endemic in *The Tenant*. Private conversations are overheard – as when Helen discovers her husband's infidelity and chooses, in an act of 'ungenerous concealment' (*TWH* 342), to keep silent; Hargrave makes his violent approach to Helen and is discovered by Hattersley, and Gilbert eavesdrops on a conversation between Lawrence and Helen. A more intricate example of this process comes in the form of Eliza's desire 'to exchange places' (*TWH* 80) with Rose in order literally to distance herself from Helen whose body Eliza regards as contaminated and not fit to be admitted into a respectable middle-class home. At other times public space is subjugated to private ends, as when both Huntington and Gilbert make use of their attendance at church as a resource to further their erotic designs upon Helen. Similarly, Hargrave plays a game of chess with Helen whose subtext is the sexual conquest over her which he has failed to achieve. This chess game serves as a spatial re-enactment of the power-struggles which are traced throughout the text.

BODILY SPACE

In *The Tenant*, Brontë also explores the boundaries which conventionally delimit subjectivity through an emphasis on the body. From the outset, Helen's identity as a respectable woman is intimately connected to the question of her body and, more specifically, her ability to regulate desire. When her aunt seeks to advise Helen on the proper course she should take as an eligible woman facing a potential suitor, she tells her to 'Keep a guard over your eyes and ears as the inlets of your heart, and over your lips as the outlet, lest they betray you in a moment of unwariness'. This advice neatly encapsulates the extent to which the unguarded body threatens to expose not only the secret longings of the 'heart' but also the dangers to which this might lead. The threat to female respectability is figured metonymically through a substitution of eyes and ears for another orifice more likely to lead women to '[fall] into snares and temptations terrible to relate'. Ironically, the aunt's use of 'lips' in this context suggests a partial failure to police her own language even as she seeks to control the words her niece might utter.

In the initial stages of her courtship with Huntington, it becomes clear that Helen fails to manage her body with the control her aunt would prefer when she advises, 'Let your eyes be blind to all external attractions, your ears deaf to all the fascinations of flattery and light discourse' (*TWH* 132). This is borne out in an illicit encounter between the two courting figures, which is interrupted by Helen's aunt with the demand that Helen stay out of public view 'till that shocking colour is somewhat abated, and your eyes have recovered something of their natural expression' (*TWH* 147). While the disarray in Helen's face betokens sexual arousal, her aunt's attempts to bring it under control have no effect except to enrage her niece. In addition to succumbing to the visual and auditory allures of the male, Helen surrenders her own experience of the sensual and intellectual world:

> In all my employments, whatever I do, or see, or hear has an ultimate reference to him; whatever skill or knowledge I acquire is some day to be turned to his advantage or amusement; whatever new beauties in nature or art I discover, are to be depicted to meet his eye, or stored in memory to be told to him at some future period. (*TWH* 152)

While Helen indulges her passion for Huntington by anticipating the vicarious pleasures he might obtain, the self-control she is meant to exert at a bodily level is challenged by the forcefulness of his approaches. The possibility that female agency might be overturned by male physical strength is not foreseen by the aunt even though she is fully aware of Huntington's disregard for the social conventions which govern interactions between the sexes, as for example when he returns from his field-sports covered in blood but nonetheless accompanies the women to the house 'to the no small offense of [Helen's] aunt's strict sense of propriety' (*TWH* 161).

Huntington uses physical force not only during courtship but also to bring it to an end. The description of Huntington's marriage proposal – his attempt 'forcibly [to possess] himself of [Helen's] hand' – stands as a figure for the violations to which his bride will implicitly be subjected. Even though Helen evades his grasp at this point, she eventually finds herself pinned by Huntington, 'kneeling on [her] dress' (*TWH* 167). Huntington's utterance, 'Will you bestow yourself upon me? – you will!', is presented as both a question and a command and accompanied by an embrace which squeezes Helen 'to death in his arms' (*TWH* 168).

Though Helen's physical and sexual assault by her husband is never directly presented in *The Tenant*, the text provides other instances of male violence in the glimpses it offers of Milicent's life with Hattersley and the attack on Helen by Hargrave, against whom she defends herself with a 'palette-knife' (*TWH* 358). Male violence towards women is even hinted at in relation to Gilbert, who gives Helens hand 'a spiteful squeeze' (*TWH* 35) when first they meet and comes eventually to doubt the value of his '*love*' for Helen since it is 'forced upon her against her will' (*TWH* 474). Elsewhere, in a particularly shocking scene, Huntington offers his wife to his assembly of male friends with the comment: 'I value her so highly that any one among you, that can fancy her, may have her and welcome – you may, by Jove and my blessing into the bargain!' (*TWH* 355). Indeed, the sexual aspect of Helen's relationship with Huntington is closed off from view. Her diary omits the period which covers their wedding and has Helen herself firmly barricade her bedroom against husband and reader alike.

Helen's desire for Huntington leads to a union which eventually dissolves her identity and leads her to assume the social conscience he lacks. She writes:

> I so identify myself with him, that I feel his degradation, his failings, and transgressions as my own; I blush for him, I fear for him; I repent for him, weep, pray, and feel for him as for myself; but I cannot act for him; and hence, I must be and I am debased, contaminated by the union, both in my own eyes, and in the actual truth. (*TWH* 262)

Admitting the limits of her influence when confronted by male agency, Helen suggests that her passion for Huntington corrodes the principles she hoped would bring about his redemption:

> I am so determined to love him – so intensely anxious to excuse his errors, that I am continually dwelling upon them, and labouring to extenuate the loosest of his principles and the worst of his practices, till I am familiarized with vice and almost a partaker in his sins. Things that formerly shocked and disgusted me now seem only natural. (*TWH* 262)

Since Helen's marriage compromises not only her subjectivity but also her moral identity, the suggestion is that her romantic idealism is a dangerous force and perhaps even leads her to collude in her own destruction.

Huntington's attempts to control the female body are reversed by Helen as she tries to curb his physical excesses 'by incessant perseverance, by kindness, and firmness, and vigilance, by coaxing, and daring, and determination' (*TWH* 260). In both cases, the body of the other is the site of a power-struggle. For Huntington the main aim is to facilitate marriage – the legally sanctioned possession by the male of the female body – whereas for Helen the goal is Huntington's social reform and spiritual redemption. Her success in this endeavour would testify, not only to the moral influence she exerts but also to the love she and Huntington have for one another. As such, Helen's reforming zeal is not simply rooted in a sense of Christian duty but in a need to see the power of sexual desire confirmed through the effects it produces.

While Helen's reformation of Huntington primarily revolves around verbal persuasion combined with attempts to isolate him (from his friends as well as herself), her interventions on behalf of their son prove to be more active. In a scene recalled by Gilbert, Helen and his mother enter into a heated exchange. The conflict concerns the relative values of temperance and abstinence, but relates, more particularly, to the question of Helen's duty to her son. Mrs Markham (whose own son is capable of petty and spectacular violence if he does not get what he desires) insists that Helen's protective stance towards her son will feminize him, while Helen maintains it is her duty to arm him against the 'temptations' which will 'assail him, both from within and without' (*TWH* 32). To this end she admits her past custom of making 'him swallow a little wine or weak spirits-and-water, by way of medicine when he was sick' (*TWH* 31). What she does not say here but describes in her diary is the practice of lacing the alcohol with 'a small quantity of tartar-emetic – just enough to produce inevitable nausea and depression without positive sickness'. The 'aversion' to which this cocktail gives rise leads Helen to deploy alcohol as a 'threat' (*TWH* 370) which effectively instils a sober obedience in her child. Mrs Markham herself comes under critical scrutiny in her son's account of her role as hostess, as he comments that she is 'too anxious to make her guests happy, thereby forcing several of them to do what their soul abhorred, in the way of eating or drinking' (*TWH* 37). Working towards very different ends, both women seek to promote the well-being of others by force-feeding (an inverted form of the programme is attempted by the men who attack

Lord Lowborough in order to put an end to his abstinence). Although this force-feeding by the women confirms their gendered position since it relates to nurturance, it suggests that they are, like the men, liable to exert their power by seeking to subdue the body of the other.

If *The Tenant* only hints at the sexual violation which threatens Helen, it is much more explicit when it comes to detailing the corporeal decay to which Huntington is subject. His hideous decline is charted throughout the course of the diary, which places considerable emphasis on 'the symptoms of a disordered frame' (*TWH* 260) and the physical effects of his indulgences. His body finally becomes a spectacle when Helen returns to nurse him through a physical crisis brought on by a riding accident. The progress of this crisis is recorded in Helen's letters to her brother, within which she both illustrates the effects of Huntington's intemperance and rehearses the theological arguments – particularly those which relate to the notion of eternal damnation – which were much debated within the various Christian factions of the day.[24] Helen's concern for the physical and spiritual well-being of another is, unsurprisingly, not shared by Gilbert, who awaits the negative outcome of Huntington's struggles in order to advance his own claims. His 'confession' (*TWH* 438) that he desires the termination of Huntington's life is one which he justifies on theological grounds. He reasons that in negotiating death 'after a warning sickness, and with such an angel [as Helen] by his side', Huntington has as much of an advantage as he deserves.

Gilbert's interest in the scene of death and its possible outcomes is shared by one of Brontë's recent critics, who contemplates the textual fulfilment of Gilbert's wish 'that it might please Heaven to remove [Huntington] to a better world' (*TWH* 439). According to Janet Kunert, the 'mortification' which invades Huntington's body on his deathbed has multiple meanings:

> Before the time of antibiotics, an accident might lead to 'mortifica-tion', a synonym for gangrene, which would be aggravated if the patient were a heavy drinker or if he persisted in drinking. In ironic justice, the patient's sufferings in both cases are those which he has brought upon himself. 'Mortification' then as now, however, also could mean the subjugation of appetites and passions – a

subjugation not unknown to Victorians. A third meaning – humiliation – was familiar, particularly to Victorian women. If women endured mortification imposed by the male-controlled milieu, in fiction they could reverse the victimization and discreetly relish the mortification of the male. Some feminine wish-fulfilment must have resided in the ambiguous term, the literal decay revenging the metaphoric humiliation.[25]

The infection which takes control of Huntington's body as a result of persistent self-violations suggests the corporeal limits to his power. Huntington's accident combines, with a last drinking bout, to bring about his demise. On his deathbed, Helen seeks to reinsert him into the conventional order by persuading him to prepare for judgement in the afterlife. Huntington's refusal to comply suggests, fittingly, that he forfeits his place in heaven just as he has compelled Helen to relinquish hers on earth.

3

A Poetics of Loss

The doubleness of women's poetry comes from its ostensible adoption of an affective mode, often simple, often pious, often conventional. But those conventions are subjected to investigation, questioned, or used for unexpected purposes. The simpler the surface of the poem, the more likely it is that a second and more difficult poem will exist beneath it.

– Isobel Armstrong[1]

The poetry of Anne Brontë readily conforms to the palimpsestual model outlined by Armstrong in the epigraph above, appearing on its surface thoroughly conventional in both form and content. First published alongside the work of her sisters, it brought satisfaction to at least one contemporary reviewer, who welcomed *Poems* by Currer, Ellis and Acton Bell (1846) with the following:

Here we have good, wholesome, refreshing, vigorous poetry – no sickly affectations, no namby-pamby, no tedious imitations of familiar strains, but original thoughts, expressed in the true language of poetry – not in its cant, as is the custom with mocking-bird poets.[2]

These comments inadvertently highlight those aspects of the poetry which subsequent commentators have found to be less laudable. Until recently, Brontë's contribution to the volume in question, along with her more extensive poetic output, has been viewed with something less than enthusiasm by her critics. As Edward Chitham notes, Brontë's 'relative lack of vivid image and metaphor, her terseness and archaic yet simple vocabulary and style, may cause her work to be dismissed by seekers after the spectacular'.[3] The apparent simplicity of Brontë's style is matched by the seemingly 'wholesome' sentiments of a poetry which focuses on the vicissitudes of emotional and spiritual life. Frequently, the poetry expresses the various crises which beset the subject and seeks to resolve them by drawing upon spiritual or religious discourses. It therefore seems to participate in what Armstrong calls the 'dominant poetics of expression'[4] in order to affirm Christian faith and the doctrines with which such faith is associated.

Critics have responded to this aspect of Brontë's poetry by placing it firmly within the Christian literary tradition and, more particularly, by tracing within it the influence of John Bunyan, George Herbert and William Cowper. Elizabeth Langland suggests, for example, that Brontë's religious poetry 'expresses a generous Christian sensibility',[5] whereas P. J. M. Scott argues that in the least successful of Brontë's devotional poems 'Christian doctrines are merely versified'.[6] Although she argues that Brontë's poetry subverts feminine ideals, Maria Frawley nonetheless suggests that its feminist project is heavily dependent upon an Evangelical rhetoric and, ultimately, upon an understanding of the 'self in relation to God'.[7]

Of all the comments on Brontë's poetry, Chitham's assertion that it constitutes a form of 'spiritual or emotional autobiography'[8] deserves particular attention. It could be argued that Chitham's phrasing conflates the spiritual with the emotional or, alternatively, that it suggests that the two distinct elements exist in a balanced relation. While Chitham certainly identifies the poetry's key elements, his formulation seems to gloss over and obscure the tensions between them. This is perhaps understandable because of the dynamic between the emotional and spiritual which operates throughout Brontë's poetry. Focusing on extreme emotional states or moments of personal crisis, Brontë's poems invariably articulate subjectivity in terms of loss, lack and absence. Within this context, spirituality is a resource to which the anguished speaker looks in order to compensate for, or at least ameliorate the pain of loss. In some of the poems, such as 'Despondency', 'Fluctuations' and 'A Hymn', it is the absence of spirituality, in the form of faith or belief, which itself constitutes the crisis the speaker faces. In others, the invocation of faith ostensibly enables the speaker to negotiate loss by drawing upon the transcendental doctrines which underpin Christianity. In this way, Christianity appears to feature as a form of recompense: it not only alleviates present grief but also enables the speaker to imagine future exaltation.

One of the ways in which the tension between the emotional and spiritual can be explored is by considering a selection of those poems in which absence is inscribed in its acutest form – death. Within these poems – 'Severed and Gone, So Many Years!', 'To —', 'To Cowper' and 'Views of Life' – the deceptive nature of Brontë's psychic economy (together with a certain suspicion of language) is at its most pronounced. The experience of grief and mourning not only drives the bereft subject to seek solace in religion but also, and more radically, calls into question the efficacy of such compensatory strategies. In this respect, the conventional religious resolutions with which Brontë so often closes her poems, thereby seeming to alleviate 'the anguish that defies relief' ('Self-Communion', line 91), can be seen to rest upon an ultimately delusive piety. The poetry gestures towards a completion which is achieved when the spiritual is called upon to resolve emotional conflict and, in so doing, conceals the extent to which the Christianity it appears thus to advocate is otherwise subjected to a more profound interrogation.

'SEVERED AND GONE, SO MANY YEARS!'

The poems discussed within this chapter focus on the relation between the emotional/earthly and spiritual/divine forces operating within and upon the bereft subject. In the first poem, 'Severed and Gone, So Many Years!' (1847), the speaker's desire to transcend the embodied self and its concerns, initially by investigating the intellectual realm and then by calling upon the divine, neither resolves the mourning process nor enables a movement beyond the physicality of death. These failures lead the speaker, at the close of the poem, to resolve the crisis brought about by loss in a way which emphasizes the power of memory to overcome division, not only between living and dead, but between earthly and spiritual realms also.

The speaker of the poem seeks, 'many years' after the death of the beloved, to find a language with which to articulate loss. Despite repeated attempts to adhere to the belief that death is a mere suspension of a particular 'form' of life, the speaker nonetheless remains fixated by loss in its physical dimension. This corporeal emphasis manifests itself not only through a woeful contemplation of the corpse of the beloved, but also through inscriptions of the effects of death on the mourning body. The first stanza abruptly establishes the intensity of the grief:

> Severed and gone, so many years!
> And art thou still so dear to me,
> That throbbing heart and burning tears
> Can witness how I clung to thee?

(lines 1–4)

Here the speaker deploys a language of sensibility to suggest that the body bears 'witness' to the effects of separation despite the length of time that has elapsed. Yet this assertion is formulated in a question which calls into doubt the veracity of the body's testament. The use of the past tense in the last line of this stanza, with the word 'clung' instead of 'cling', implies that the speaker no longer exists in a dependent relation to the beloved. This in turn produces a dissonance as the bond between mourner and mourned is consigned to the past even as the effects of the grief continue to be registered by 'throbbing heart and burning tears'. The question posed within the stanza relates to the extent to which the embodied self can be said to provide an adequate record of what has been lost. At the same time that the body as 'witness' to the past is called into question, the speaker wonders whether the effects and affects it continues to suffer can 'still' be read as the sign of a bond unbroken.

As if to confirm the distrust of the body and its emotions, the second and third stanzas, each beginning with the phrase 'I know', focus on the speaker's intellectual comprehension:

> I know that in the narrow tomb
> The form I loved was buried deep,
> And left, in silence and in gloom,
> To slumber out its dreamless sleep.
>
> I know the corner, where it lies,
> Is but a dreary place of rest:
> The charnel moisture never dries
> From the dark flagstones o'er its breast

(lines 5–12)

With their emphasis on what is known rather than felt, these stanzas suggest a rejection of the uncertainties of Armstrong's 'affective mode'. Such a transition from the somatic to the cerebral proves to be compromised, however, because the knowledge which the speaker advances still relates to the body – albeit the body of the dead. These first stanzas encapsulate the contrary movement of the poem as a whole, as it repeatedly tries to articulate loss in non-corporeal terms and consistently fails to do so.

The two stanzas cited immediately above each begin by registering the speaker's knowledge of the physical dimension to death. More specifically, each concerns the disposal of a 'form' which, as the words 'it' and 'its' would suggest, has passed from subject to object. While the first three lines of the poem's second stanza equate burial with the neglect or abandonment of the dead, the speaker resorts, particularly in the last line, to a euphemistic language which momentarily lays to rest the anxiety which this equation articulates. Even so, the language of euphemism proves to be contradictory: 'slumber' and 'sleep' hold out the possibility of a subjectivity persisting beyond death even as the word 'dreamless' works to annihilate it.

The failure of the poem's euphemistic strategies prompts the speaker's return, in stanza three, to the site of burial. This stanza also echoes, with the words 'but a dreary place of rest', the earlier attempt to construct death as a mere hiatus between life and afterlife. Taken together, stanzas two and three indicate that the speaker's anxiety concerning death is double, as the fear of the absolute negation of the subject is accompanied by the fear of entrapment within a tomb. There is a sense in which the speaker also suffers a kind of entrapment within the poem itself: the language which is supposed to lay the dead to rest raises the spectral possibility that the beloved, far from being 'Severed and gone', is simply and permanently caught in a condition of incarceration. The speaker's unease with regard to these possibilities is compounded by what is perhaps a more troubling and gruesome misgiving that the beloved is neither negated nor incarcerated but decomposing. The decompositional process is figured in lines 11–12, through a seepage of flesh into air: 'The charnel moisture never dries/From the dark flagstones o'er its breast'. It is also suggested syntactically as the sentence which opens the third stanza is not concluded until the close of the fourth:

> For there the sunbeams never shine,
> Nor ever breathes the freshening air,
> – But not for this do I repine;
> For my beloved is not there.

(lines 13–16)

In this way the body defies the attempts to conceal its decomposition carried out by 'tomb' and poem alike.

While the use of euphemism in the poem apparently works to conceal the effects of corporeal decay, it also introduces a spiritual dimension into the poem. In stanza four, the speaker seeks again to move away from the body by deploying a language which removes the beloved from its place of rest. This tactic enables the speaker to claim that the grief which is articulated does not relate to the physical decay and apparent deprivations the body suffers. The protestation which opens stanza five neatly encapsulates the poem's attempt to move beyond the materiality of death and its simultaneous failure to do so:

> O, no! I do not think of thee
> As festering there in slow decay: –
> 'Tis this sole thought oppresses me,
> That thou art gone so far away.

(lines 17–20)

That the speaker does indeed think of the corruption of the flesh is evidenced in the detail of the second line. The last two lines of this stanza represent another attempt to check the morbid fixation upon the body of the dead, this time by emphasizing the distance which separates the mourner from the beloved. Although this distance is vaguely couched in the words 'thou art gone so far away', the following stanza confirms that what separates the speaker from the dead is the distance between heaven and earth:

> For ever gone; for I, by night,
> Have prayed, within my silent room,
> That Heaven would grant a burst of light
> Its cheerless darkness to illume

(lines 21–4)

While this stanza, like the two preceding verses, appears to assert a belief in a Christian afterlife, it opens by insisting nonetheless that separation through death is final, in a phrase which is itself provocatively marked by the absence of a grammatical subject: 'For ever gone'. This insistence is supported by the fact that, despite the speaker's heavenly supplications, the beloved does not return to earth, even momentarily. The logic which underpins the finality of 'For ever gone' appears then to relate not only to the physical absence of the dead, but also encompasses the spiritual division between mourner and mourned. Far from anticipating a celestial reunion with the beloved, the speaker assumes that the gap between living and dead can only be bridged on earth. This secular emphasis implies that the distance between mourner and mourned also constitutes a gulf between the damned and the saved. The speaker cites as evidence of the finality of these separations the fact that the prayers – directed towards 'Heaven' and the beloved – which might facilitate the return of the dead, go unanswered. The ambiguity of this stanza allows the unanswered status of the prayers to be read in two ways. Either the silence with which they meet confirms an apparent lack of spiritual worth or, alternatively, suggests that the speaker must abandon the faith in which the prayers are grounded. Both possibilities accentuate the division between speaker and beloved.

As the poem unfolds, the speaker's bodily fixation becomes increasingly apparent. Not only does s/he return to the body of the dead and its place of burial but also tries to resurrect the body through prayer. While this strategy is unsuccessful, it nonetheless enables a return, in stanzas six to ten, to the embodied self and its expressions. These stanzas provide a record of the speaker's attempt to bring about a restoration – albeit fleeting – of the dead. Since the speaker tries to facilitate this process through prayer, the poem seems to redramatize the desire to move beyond the corporeal, in the form of a call for divine intervention. However, since what the speaker prays for is the return of the beloved in a physical shape, the use of prayer to achieve this end seems revealingly inappropriate. This becomes apparent in the shift in the poem's rhetoric which occurs between stanzas six and seven. Although the speaker prays for 'a burst of light' to illuminate both the night and the silence of the room, such a spiritual idiom becomes enmeshed in a language of bodily desire, as prayer turns into fantasy. The clear poetic and psychic investment which this fantasy receives indicates an overturning of spiritual and carnal hierarchies:

> And give thee to my longing eyes,
> A moment, as thou shinest now,
> Fresh from thy mansion in the skies,
> With all its glories on thy brow.
>
> Wild was the wish, intense the gaze
> I fixed upon the murky air,
> Expecting, half, a kindling blaze
> Would strike my raptured vision there, –
>
> A shape these human nerves would thrill,
> A majesty that might appal,
> Did not thy earthly likeness, still,
> Gleam softly, gladly, through it all.

(lines 25–36)

The language of these three stanzas is grounded in an opposition between light and heat, on the one hand, and darkness on the other, and seems therefore to rely upon a Christian discourse of enlightenment. Both heaven and the beloved are endowed here with the power to illuminate the 'cheerless darkness' the mourner inhabits. Yet the visionary experience which the speaker outlines ultimately gratifies the embodied rather than spiritual self. The 'Wild ... wish' of line 29 is granted a noticeably scopophilic satisfaction: 'longing eyes'; 'intense ... gaze'; 'raptured vision'.

The problem with the bodily rapture envisaged here is that it threatens to overwhelm the speaker's senses as the poem's eroticism assumes a distinctly gothic cast, invoking 'murky air' that in turn reveals 'A shape these human nerves would thrill,/ A majesty that might appal'. Although the stanzas appear to confirm the forcefulness of the visionary experience, they also disclose the power of earthly desires. While the 'raptured vision' is situated 'there' and thus placed outside the speaker, the phrase simultaneously points to a state of erotic entrancement. The suggestion emerges that the moment of illumination has a sexual rather than spiritual origin and that the life of fantasy has the capacity to terrorize. In seeking to escape this violent predicament the speaker attempts, in stanza nine, to discover within it the familiar. The 'earthly likeness', which 'Gleams softly, gladly, through it all', counteracts the demonic excess the speaker has conjured. The word 'gladly' refers not only to the 'earthly likeness' but also describes the speaker's response to the respite its presence offers. This doubling of the speaker and the beloved through the syntax is also underlined at the beginning of the stanza, as 'A shape these human nerves could thrill' can be read in two ways. The 'thrill' can either refer to the effect the 'shape' produces on the speaker or, alternatively, the effect 'these human nerves' might have on the 'shape'. This doubling suggests that the speaker is not simply acted upon within the realms of fantasy but is able also to act upon another.

Since the speaker's prayer is not answered except insofar as it is displaced by a fantasy which allows for the voicing of desire, stanza eleven sees the speaker look elsewhere for other signs of the beloved's presence. The attempt to conjure the beloved yields to a fetishistic contemplation of objects which stand in for the dead. Yet these tokens, 'one shining tress' (line 41) and 'a pictured form' (line 43), which might otherwise enable remembrance are not in possession of the speaker who longs for the visual satisfaction they might provide. Their absence leads the speaker to return to the physical traces of the beloved, the remains of the dead which dominate the early section of the poem:

> A few cold words on yonder stone,
> A corpse as cold as they can be –
> Vain words, and mouldering dust, alone –
> Can this be all that's left of thee?
>
> O, no! Thy spirit lingers still
> Where'er thy sunny smile was seen:
> There's less of darkness, less of chill
> On earth, than if thou hadst not been.

(lines 45–52)

Revisiting the scene of the burial, these stanzas repeat but also modify the protestation first made in stanza five as the 'spirit' of the beloved is said to '[linger] still' 'On earth' rather than be located 'far away'. The reference to the 'few cold words on yonder stone' stands in direct contrast to the language of the earlier visionary stanzas and the 'kindling blaze' the speaker has invoked with her/his own testament to the beloved. Brontë's use of the word 'Vain' at this juncture points (as in 'Views of Life', line 5) to the failure of language adequately to convey a sense of loss as well as the self-centred nature of such loss. As if in an attempt to move beyond the personal terms in which the loss has hitherto been articulated, the speaker closes the poem by seeking to uncover traces of the other not only within the self but within the wider world. In stanza thirteen the 'sunny smile' of the beloved both lights and warms the earth. In stanza fourteen the speaker retreats once more into the first-person mode and incorporates the lost other back into the physical self:

> Thou breathest in my bosom yet,
> And dwellest in my beating heart;
> And, while I cannot quite forget,
> Thou, darling, canst not quite depart.

> (lines 53–6)

In this way, the speaker suggests that the body originally afflicted at the poem's opening now derives its own vitality from the beloved. Equally, the memory the speaker retains of the beloved ensures that the dead cannot leave the earth. From this perspective, mourner and mourned appear to be united in a symbiosis forged through recollection. In stanza fifteen the speaker asserts the wider sphere of influence the beloved continues to have on humanity through the collective 'us' (line 60). The poem's penultimate stanza is perhaps the most affirmative of all. It privileges the effects the beloved has had on the speaker's own perception of 'Life' and 'men' (lines 61, 62), thus undercutting the loss and negation which has predominated within the mourning process.

It is significant that these last attempts to reconcile the self to loss emphasize the earthly traces left by the beloved rather than the compensations of paradise. They lead the speaker to claim, in stanzas fourteen and fifteen, that the beloved's ascension to heaven is not fully accomplished: this 'darling' 'canst not quite depart' and is 'not riven' from earthly dwellers. In the final stanza, the speaker insists:

> Earth hath received thine earthly part;
> Thine heavenly flame has heavenward flown;
> But both still linger in my heart,
> Still live, and not in mine alone.

> (lines 65–8)

With these words the speaker returns with a renewed faith to the 'heart' which, in stanza one, first bore 'witness' to loss. The poem negotiates loss, not by drawing upon spiritual solace, but by finally affirming the validity of the embodied self as a memorial to the other. Here, the speaker's 'heart' is not only capable of bridging the divide between living and dead through remembrance but, in so doing, and more significantly, it also subverts one of the principal tenets of Christian doctrine, gathering the dead back into itself, body and soul.

'TO —'

The pattern which emerges in 'Severed and Gone, So Many Years!' through the speaker's attempts and failures to transcend the limits of the body and its emotional concerns is also traced in 'To —' (1842). The speaker of this poem first begins by repudiating the mourning process by drawing upon a language which naturalizes death:

> I will not mourn thee, lovely one,
>   Though thou art torn away.
> 'Tis said that if the morning sun
>   Arise with dazzling ray
>
> And shed a bright and burning beam
>   Athwart the glittering main,
> 'Ere noon shall fade that laughing gleam
>   Engulfed in clouds and rain.

(lines 1–8)

The speaker announces in the first two lines a paradoxical refusal to acknowledge the departure of the 'lovely one'. Yet the psychic posture adopted here proves fragile. The dual metaphor of sun and rain – signifying life and death respectively – functions as a means of placing the loss of an individual within the larger context of a natural cycle. However, the words ''Tis said', which introduce the metaphor, suggest that it represents a consolatory truism from which the speaker remains distant. As if to signal the failure of a conventionalized language of consolation, the poem performs a deconstruction of the sun/rain opposition. Far from representing an unequivocal life-force, the 'morning sun', as the homonym suggests, already carries within itself the shadow of loss. Additionally, insofar as the sun 'shed[s] a bright and burning beam', the poem hints, from the outset, at a falling away and depletion of powers. The subsequent fading of the 'laughing gleam' is thus forecast by Brontë's language. The 'gleam' does not even last until sunset, but is eclipsed at the very moment – noon – at which it should touch its zenith. The cumulative effect of these linguistic disturbances is to produce an identification between sun and speaker, rather than between the sun and the beloved for whom it should stand in. Like the speaker, the sun fails to transcend the 'clouds and rain' which are traditionally associated with low spirits. Both figures are 'Engulfed' by grief.

The speaker's acceptance of a metaphor designed to lessen the impact of loss is stated ambivalently in these opening stanzas. In the three which follow, the sun-figure is taken up and further explored in a spiritual context. This supplementary strategy, which attempts to show how the natural and spiritual orders reflect each other, suggests at the same time that the original metaphor is itself inadequate:

> And if thy life as transient proved,
>   It hath been full as bright,
> For thou wert hopeful and beloved;
>   Thy spirit knew no blight.
>
> If few and short the joys of life
>   That thou on earth couldst know,
> Little thou knew'st of sin and strife
>   Nor much of pain and woe.
>
> If vain thy earthly hopes did prove,
>   Thou canst not mourn their flight;
> Thy brightest hopes were fixed above
>   And they shall know no blight.

(lines 9–20)

The repetition of the word 'If' in these stanzas underlines the speaker's scepticism as s/he tries to adapt a platitude to suit the particularity of the life which has been lost. In stanza three, the shortness of the life in question is equated with the transience of the sun's power, while hope, love and purity of spirit are identified with its brilliance. These simple equations are undercut in stanzas four and five which double back to stanza three. The fourth stanza suggests a short life ensures spiritual purity only because it excludes both knowledge and experience and the suffering they bring. The curtailment of the life of the beloved is, in stanza five, offset by an accelerated promotion to the realm of the spirit. Although the beloved's 'earthly hopes' are not fulfilled, a spiritual transcendence is achieved through death. Thus, the beloved, unlike the earth-bound speaker, 'canst not mourn'. The compensatory benefits of a short life would therefore seem only to pertain, if at all, to the one who has died rather than those left behind to contemplate the momentary brilliance of that life. This logic again directs attention to the poem's dawning metaphor. I have already suggested that this metaphor has a double significance since it is used conventionally to stand in for the brevity of life but is articulated in a language which also encapsulates the experience of the mourner 'Engulfed' by loss. In this light, stanzas three to five, which somewhat perversely focus on the advantages of an early death, simply highlight the limited use to which rhetorical or literary conventions can be put. The compensations offered to the beloved upon death are not shared by the one who remains and is able to perceive the loss from a different perspective. It is this perspective which is offered in the poem's final four stanzas.

In stanza six, the speaker, having considered the arguments which are designed to obviate the need to mourn, returns to the mode of the first-person singular. At this juncture, the speaker's refusal to mourn breaks down. The previous attempts to rationalize loss and so suspend the mourning process are displaced by a belated articulation of grief:

> And yet I cannot check my sighs,
>   Thou wert so young and fair,
> More bright than summer morning skies,
>   But stern death would not spare

(lines 21–4)

Here, the luminosity of the beloved outshines even the sun in its role as a source of metaphorical comfort. The use of the sun-metaphor at this point and in the next stanza would seem to represent an example of one of the techniques Armstrong associates with Brontë who, she argues, 'negotiated the sobriety of the religious and didactic lyric to suggest precisely where its conventions are most painful and intransigent by *not* breaking these conventions, but by simply following through their logic'.[9]

Having sought to incorporate the sun-figure into the poem as a means of rationalizing and screening loss, Brontë finally stages a direct confrontation with a personified death. In stanza seven, beloved and sun are fused together through the trope of a 'shining eye' (line 27) and extinguished alike by a greater power:

> He would not pass our darling by
> Nor grant one hour's delay,
> But rudely closed his shining eye
> And frowned his smile away

(lines 25–8)

Here death dispenses both with an inadequate metaphor and the beloved simultaneously. As if to underscore this point, death outlives the stanza while the sun does not. In stanza eight, the negating effects of death are figured through the eradication of the beloved's 'angel smile' (line 29) and the silencing of the 'music' of his 'voice' (line 32). In this stanza, the speaker abandons the sun-figure and tries to define what is individual about the lost other by switching to a different register. The beloved is depicted in an idiom which articulates the speaker's own perception of him rather than through an externally imposed language. The speaker's admission of the subjective nature of loss is further signalled by the shift from the collective 'our darling' of stanza seven (where the sun-metaphor is still in play) to 'my fond heart' (line 30) in stanza eight. This leads the poem to its conclusion:

> I'll weep no more thine early doom,
> But O! I still must mourn
> The pleasures buried in thy tomb,
> For they will not return.

(lines 33–6)

The opening line of this stanza appears to consolidate the speaker's initial stance (the refusal to mourn). Yet at the same time it exposes the flaws in that stance because in claiming to 'weep no more' the speaker implies that tears have already been shed. Although the speaker may have exhausted the sorrow prompted by the 'early doom' of the beloved, the rest of the stanza revives grief while gesturing towards its additional and more pressing source. In the penultimate line of the poem, the word 'pleasures' indicates that the language deployed by the speaker in the previous stanza only touches upon the surfaces of loss. It is unclear whether the 'pleasures buried' are those which the beloved ought to enjoy or ones now held out of the speaker's reach. In either case, the poem makes a last-minute disclosure of unspecified sensual and erotic delights whose loss is irrevocable. It becomes clear that the 'pleasures' buried in the tomb of the beloved have also always lain submerged within the poem, which thus at once takes on the aspects of crypt and cryptogram. The final loss suffered by the speaker is a linguistic one: no sooner does the poem admit to 'pleasures' that are themselves already vague, than it is suddenly arrested.

If the two closing stanzas of the poem point to a movement of resistance and counter-resistance, as an original refusal is displaced by a compulsion to mourn, they also return the reader to the poem's title, 'To —'. The convention which demands that the identity of the beloved remain undisclosed is – in the erasure which it performs – an appropriate one. Yet, as the poem's conclusion illustrates, the conventions Brontë invokes are at the same time to some degree circumvented as the hitherto repressed desires of mourner and mourned come into view.

'TO COWPER'

If the conventional reticence of 'To —' is called into question by its close, the next poem seems to allow a public statement of intimacy and connection to be articulated. In 'To Cowper' (1842) the speaker establishes an allegiance with the eighteenth-century poet, based on a process of identification in which the speaker's own sense of loss is read in the writing of the other. Yet even as the poem dramatizes such a process, its central concern is to raise questions about the limits of identification itself.

Stanza one recalls the work of the 'Celestial Bard' in a language which not only suggests a communion between reader and writer but also highlights the double-edged nature of their joint concerns:

71

> Sweet are thy strains, Celestial Bard,
> And oft in childhood's years
> I've read them o'er and o'er again
> With floods of silent tears.

(lines 1–4)

Though 'Sweet', the poet's articulations are designated as 'strains', a word which indicates both the melodious form the poet adopts and the struggle and labour it entails. By the same token, the speaker as child derives repeated but paradoxical pleasure from one whose work nonetheless facilitates 'floods of silent tears'. Such a cathartic effect is 'traced' in the second stanza to the speaker's narcissistic identification with the language of the poet:

> The language of my inmost heart
> I traced in every line –
> *My* sins, *my* sorrows, hopes and fears
> Were there, and only mine.

(lines 5–8)

The speaker takes possession of the poet's words, finding within them a reflection of self which is so pronounced that even their originator is effaced. This is an effect that the poem will go on to re-evaluate, principally by considering the ways in which such an extreme identification obscures the original traumas out of which Cowper's work emerges. Yet this attempt to acknowledge the other fails in its turn. While the speaker eventually comes to recognize the other's autonomy, such a recognition is ultimately subordinated to egocentric ends.

In stanzas three and four, the speaker moderates the initial enthusiastic reception – and appropriation – of the poet's work. This reassessment begins with the admission, in stanza three, of the conceited pleasure the poetry generates:

> All for myself the sigh would swell,
> The tear of anguish start;
> I little knew what wilder woe
> Had filled the poet's heart.
>
> I did not know the nights of gloom,
> The days of misery,
> The long long years of dark despair
> That crushed and tortured thee.

(lines 9–16)

In the first two lines of stanza three, the words 'swell' and 'tear' not only indicate bodily responses to the recognition which the poet's language bestows upon the suffering speaker, but also highlight the dangers such recognition entails. The speaker's expressive response threatens not only to overwhelm but also breach or 'tear' the subject. This threat is diminished and therefore contained by the following two lines of the stanza, in which the speaker admits the poet's own anguish or 'wilder woe'. Such an acknowledgement of the greater intensity which characterizes Cowper's subjective experience is curiously ambiguous because it suggests that the language which articulates this experience, and/or the process of its interpretation, somehow erases the authorial subject himself. As the speaker goes on, in stanza four, to speculate on the emotional turmoil which gives rise to the poet's utterances, Brontë's own language becomes increasingly oppressive. The 'wilder woe' the poet endures would seem not only to fill his 'heart' but threaten him with annihilation. If the poet's work induces a dangerous catharsis in the speaker, he himself is granted no such release.

In stanza five, the speaker records the poet's eventual death and the return of his 'gentle soul' to 'God' and 'Home' alike (lines 18, 19, 20). In so doing, s/he carries out the very liberation which Cowper's own work could not provide. This stanza not only represents the poet's departure from 'earth' (line 17) and heavenly ascension but also constitutes a textual transition in its own right. It marks out the distance between the first four stanzas, which emphasize the respective sufferings of speaker and poet, and the six stanzas to follow, which take up the question of spiritual redemption. If, however, this transitional stanza puts an unequivocal end to Cowper's suffering, its assertion of his salvation is far less certain.

In the last six stanzas the speaker's language becomes more tentative and questioning, and suggestive, as such, of the ambivalence which frequently informs Brontë's inscriptions of Christian faith. What is important in this poem is that the speaker's desire to confirm the poet's salvation is less altruistic than it at first seems. The speaker draws upon a knowledge of Christian doctrine in order to determine, not only the poet's final destination, but also her/his own. In stanza six, for example, Cowper's fate seems inextricably bound up with that of the speaker:

It must be so if God is love
And answers fervent prayer;
Then surely thou shalt dwell on high,
And I may meet thee there.

(lines 21–4)

This piously anticipated reunion depends upon a God who fulfils the speaker's expectations. It is therefore conditional upon a language which accurately conveys the identity of God and is accurately interpreted by the speaker. Yet the words 'if' and 'may' ensure that the Christian doctrine with which this stanza resonates does not go unchallenged. In stanzas seven to ten the Christian rhetoric in which the speaker is enmeshed – and yet doubts – becomes more explicit:

Is He the source of every good,
The spring of purity?
Then in thine hours of deepest woe
Thy God was still with thee.

How else when every hope was fled
Couldst thou so fondly cling
To holy things and holy men
And how so sweetly sing –

Of things that God alone could teach?
And whence that purity;
That hatred of all sinful ways,
That gentle Charity?

Are these the symptoms of a heart
Of Heavenly grace bereft,
For ever banished from its God,
To Satan's fury left?

(lines 25–40)

In this sequence, the speaker identifies in the poet's language evidence supporting the presence of God and in this way seems able to answer the question of lines 25–6 in the affirmative. The speaker then goes on to argue that the poet's words are themselves 'the symptoms of a heart' precisely not 'Of Heavenly grace bereft'. As the speaker advances this logic, in which the poet becomes a kind of mirror to God, the reader's attention is drawn back to the initial identification between poet and speaker. The opening of the second stanza, in which the speaker reads 'the language of [the] inmost heart' in Cowper's work, is reflected in the opening of stanza ten.

At this juncture, the speaker's initial erasure of the poet from the poetry is redressed as the 'symptoms' of Cowper's heart become the means for deciphering his spiritual identity and destiny. The rhetorical question the speaker asks in stanza ten would seem then to be answered by this divine diagnosis and decoding of the poetry. Yet this belated reading of Cowper's Christian spirituality is at odds with the third and fourth stanzas of the poem which emphasize the condition of anguish in which the poet lives. (Indeed, the term 'symptoms' itself ironically suggests a state of ongoing 'dis-ease'). In these stanzas the poet is noticeably separated from God, a point which is underscored in stanza five, when death ends exile by facilitating a return to 'Home'.

In the poem's last stanza the speaker's contemplation of the poet's fate is revealed to be as narcissistic as the rapture with which s/he had initially greeted Cowper's work:

> Yet should thy darkest fears be true,
>   If Heaven be so severe
> That such a soul as thine is lost,
>   O! how should I appear?

(lines 41–4)

Spiritual anxiety is projected here from speaker to poet and, in a sense, located outside the poem itself. This strategy suggests an attempt to extricate self from other by safely ascribing the 'darkest fears' to Cowper. Yet the 'fears' are no sooner banished than they return in the recognition that the possibility of Cowper's damnation guarantees that of the speaker.

The final word with which the poem ends – 'appear' – is worth dwelling on. In the context of this poem, the speaker at first precisely seems to 'appear' in the language of the poet whose words reflect her/his 'inmost heart'. As this initial situation is revised during the course of the poem, the speaker would again 'appear' to have transcended egocentric concerns, even as this appearance is, in turn, shown, by the poem's close, to be deceptive.

What the poem finally shows is that its public status as a commemoration of Cowper should perhaps more properly be regarded as a means through which the speaker's own mortality and spiritual crisis are explored. This connects it to other poems in which Brontë contemplates both the life and death of the self more directly. These include 'A Hymn', 'O God! If this indeed be all' and, especially, Brontë's last poem, 'A dreadful darkness closes in', which is conventionally read autobiographically. However, the particular significance of 'To Cowper' resides in the way in which Brontë appropriates poetic conventions to her own ends. She makes use of Cowper and his work, not simply in order to assert spiritual and poetic allegiances but also to advance, along with her speaker, a different and more subversively subjective project.

'VIEWS OF LIFE'

In one of her longer poems, 'Views of Life' (1845), Brontë establishes a dialogue in which questions of grief and mourning are given another inflection. The poem unfolds as a response to an imaginary critic and revolves around the notion of a difference of perception between speaker and addressee. This difference is articulated in the first three stanzas:

> When sinks my heart in hopeless gloom,
> When life can shew no joy for me,
> And I behold a yawning tomb
> Where bowers and palaces should be,
>
> In vain, you talk of morbid dreams,
> In vain, you gaily smiling say
> That what to me so dreary seems
> The healthy mind deems bright and gay.
>
> I too have smiled, and thought like you,
> But madly smiled, and falsely deemed:
> My present thoughts I know are true,
> I'm waking now, 'twas then I dreamed.

(lines 1–12)

Brontë here offers a critique of the inability of the addressee, who does not yet feature in this one-sided dialogue, to bridge the divide between two different outlooks. The addressee in the poem appears to conflate the speaker's perspective with a state of unreality, figured both through 'morbid dreams' and the more subtle implication that the speaker's mind is perverted (lines 7–8). The speaker responds by reversing the opposition between dream and reality – 'I'm waking now, 'twas then I dreamed' – and by insisting that the pleasures which govern the addressee's viewpoint are themselves grounded in an illusion which borders on the insane. Although the speaker admits to once sharing in the optimism of the other, such optimism is recalled through memories which lend authority to the position which the speaker has now come to adopt. In contrast to the addressee, whose failed rhetoric and egocentricism are alike articulated through the repetition of 'In vain', the speaker is able to lay claim to the experiences of the other. Such an ability becomes an important part of the overall rhetorical strategy adopted by the speaker. Experience eventually becomes the dominant force in the poem and is personified as a female figure capable of utilizing narrative as a heuristic device.

Prior to this point, however, the competing claims of speaker and addressee are revealed through images which epitomize experience and hope respectively. For the speaker, the optimist's supposedly 'healthy mind' is associated with conventional literary scenes largely derived from the romance tradition. The 'bowers and palaces' of this imaginative land-scape fail to materialize in the speaker's own consciousness because it is dominated by 'a yawning tomb'. This tomb appears elsewhere in the poem as 'The bed of death' (line 47) and 'the grave' (line 64) which closes over an unsuspecting lover. The seductions of the 'bowers and palaces' are resisted by the speaker, who refuses to allow fantasy to screen out death. The speaker's resistance to romance simultaneously connotes a scepticism on Brontë's part towards its 'flattering Falsehood' (line 36) and the masking of experience for which it is responsible.

In stanzas four to seven the speaker recalls a recent visionary experience which is as deceptive as it is transient. It is conveyed through a language which itself seems limited:

> I lately saw a sunset sky,
> And stood enraptured to behold
> Its various hues of glorious dye:
> First, fleecy clouds of shining gold;

These blushing took a rosy hue;
Beneath them shone a flood of green,
Nor less divine the glorious blue
That smiled above them and between:

I cannot name each lovely shade,
I cannot say how bright they shone;
But one by one I saw them fade,
And what remained when they were gone?

Dull clouds remained of sombre hue,
And when their borrowed charm was o'er,
The sky grew dull and charmless too
That smiled so softly bright before.

(lines 13–28)

Although the speaker literally colours these stanzas with the 'varied hues of glorious dye' which characterize the 'sunset sky', these descriptive gestures eventually fail. Since language cannot fully record and translate experience, it undermines the authority with which memory is otherwise imbued. The temporary seductions of the vision and the language with which it is recalled both dissolve when a 'world of woes' (line 34) intrudes. The 'yawning tomb' continues to dictate perception because the experience which might sustain a different outlook is only fleeting and mediated 'Through all the haze of golden light/That flattering Falsehood round it throws' (lines 35–6).

In stanza nine a 'keener sight' (line 33) is reasserted and becomes the filter through which the scenes in the subsequent verses are described (stanzas ten to seventeen). These scenes feature a mother and child and two lovers, representing maternal love and sexual desire respectively. The mother, whose bond with her child is figured 'through tears of speechless rapture' (line 40), is, like the speaker, unable to articulate experience through language. However, lacking the speaker's insight, this 'Fond dreamer' is 'blinded' (lines 41, 45) by 'the object of her joy' (line 44). She does not anticipate the 'burning woe' (line 43) to which she will be exposed because of her capacity for love. The lovers who appear in the scene which follows are equally unaware of the pains to which the present fulfilment of their desires will give rise. The speaker insists that, even if their 'mutual love supremely blest' (line 50) survives subsequent 'adversity and pain' (line 55), their separation through death is inevitable. Even though the speaker concedes that the claims of 'love and faith' (line 53) represent 'The greatest blessings life can show' (line 54), the latter are suspended in parenthesis. In this way, the poem's form lends additional authority to the perceptions of the speaker.

In these scenes the poem appears to shift away from the experience of the individual speaker with which it opens, moving out to embrace the lives of imaginary others. Insofar as these lives will be claimed by the 'yawning tomb', they substantiate the perceptions of the speaker, whose subjectivity is equally constructed in relation to that dismal destination.

The poem proceeds with a second and equally one-sided dialogue, occasioned by the death of 'Pleasure', in which experience (line 70) and 'Hope' (line 75) are personified. Both figures compete over another personified figure, 'youth', in their attempt to persuade him of the validity of their respective positions:

> O, youth may listen patiently,
> While sad experience tells her tale;
> But doubt sits smiling in his eye,
> For ardent hope will still prevail.
>
> He hears how feeble Pleasure dies,
> By guilt destroyed, and pain and woe;
> He turns to Hope —and she replies
> 'Believe it not – it is not so!'
>
> (lines 69–76)

While 'youth' is male, the forces which exert their claims on him are both designated female. From the perspective of experience, Hope is both seductress and deceiver, promising pleasures endlessly deferred:

> 'O! Heed her not,' experience says,
> 'For thus she whispered once to me;
> She told me in my youthful days
> How glorious manhood's prime would be.
>
> (lines 77–80)

Since experience is female it is evident that the 'glorious manhood' promised by Hope relates to the prospect of sexual fulfilment. Hope's promises are subsequently traced through the seasons which, as they pass, become infused with an increasing melancholy. The traditional association of Spring with renewal is undercut because its coming exhausts nature itself:

> But when beneath that scorching sky
> I languished weary through the day
> While birds refused to sing,
> Verdure decayed from field and tree,
> And panting nature mourned with me
> The freshness of the spring.

(lines 95–100)

With these lines, nature and experience unite to mourn a sexuality which has fallen into decay because it has not been adequately nourished. Thus, experience proves Hope to be both liar and cheat and serves a warning to youth. While the response of 'youth' to this warning is not directly given in the poem, it is nonetheless articulated by the imaginary addressee, whose voice at last surfaces in stanza twenty-eight and dominates the remainder of the poem.

In the poem's last ten stanzas, the addressee appears to acknowledge the persuasiveness of the case made both by the poem's speaker and the personified figure of experience. Yet at the same time the ameliorative effects of Hope are not wholly relinquished. The addressee admits 'the damps of truth' (line 124) but still chooses to value Hope's illusions. The prospect of death, which informs the speaker's world-view, is recognized by the addressee but becomes a means of advancing still another perspective. This perspective sees the addressee anticipating the 'bliss' (line 170) which comes only after death in confirmation of the Christian promise of everlasting life. However, the addressee only arrives at this stance by admitting that the 'joys' previously celebrated are 'empty, frail at best' (line 126). The addressee significantly alters his/her optimism and is forced to look beyond the transient pleasures of the secular world. Taking on the 'pilgrim's woes' (line 165), the addressee confronts the prospect of the 'yawning tomb' by drawing upon Christian images of salvation.

Although these images close the poem with an apparently triumphant resolution, they also bring it full circle by recalling the problems of visionary experience explored earlier (lines 13–28). In this light – or 'false light' (line 32) – it would seem that the addressee has simply substituted conventional Christian doctrine for 'bowers and palaces', repeating one compensatory gesture with another. Like the speaker, the addressee recognizes mortality, yet only as the prelude to its transcendence. For both parties, though in different ways, the most powerful rhetorical device at their disposal, it transpires, is death.

Notes

INTRODUCTION

1. One reviewer identifies both *Agnes Grey* and *Wuthering Heights* as 'two tales so nearly related to *Jane Eyre* in cast of thought, incident and language as to excite some curiosity' before going on to identify *Agnes Grey* as the 'more acceptable...though less powerful' of the two. See unsigned review, *Athenaeum*, 25 December 1847, 1324–5; *CH* 218–19. Another critic also recognizes 'a distinct family likeness between these two tales' and notes their resemblance to *Jane Eyre*. Praising Anne's ability to reveal the 'secrets' of the governess's 'prison-house', the critic nonetheless insists that her 'heroine is a sort of younger sister to *Jane Eyre*; but inferior to her in every way'. See unsigned review, *Douglas Jerrold's Weekly Newspaper*, 15 January 1848, 77; *CH* 227.
2. For a more detailed discussion of this point see Elizabeth Langland, *Anne Brontë: The Other One* (Basingstoke: Macmillan, 1989).
3. Ibid., 154. See Winifred Gérin, *Anne Brontë* (London: Allen Lane, 1959). The problems with Gérin's autobiographical reading of *Agnes Grey* are directly addressed by Edward Chitham in *A Life of Anne Brontë* (Oxford and Cambridge, MA: Blackwell, 1991).
4. Charlotte Brontë, 'Biographical Notice of Ellis and Acton Bell', *AG* 55.
5. Terry Eagleton, for example, argues that both *Agnes Grey* and *The Tenant* 'work on the simple assumption that love, earnestness and evangelical truth are preferable to social achievement and can, with sufficient long-suffering, be attained'. While conceding that she is 'remarkably unsmug', Eagleton's final evaluation is that 'The language of Anne Brontë's work is that of morality rather than imagination' and, in his view at least, it has little purchase on the social. Terry Eagleton, *Myths of Power: A Marxist Study of the Brontës* (London and Basingstoke: Macmillan, 1975), 123, 124, 137.
6. Langland, *Anne Brontë*, 29.

7. Jill L. Matus, *Unstable Bodies: Victorian Representations of Sexuality and Maternity* (Manchester and New York: Manchester University Press, 1995), 89.

8. Susan Meyer, 'Words on "Great Vulgar Sheets"': Writing and Social Resistance in Anne Brontë's *Agnes Grey* (1847)', in Barbara Leah Harman and Susan Meyer (eds), *The New Nineteenth Century: Feminist Readings of Underread Victorian Fiction* (New York and London: Garland, 1996), 8.

9. Ibid., 4.

CHAPTER 1.   GOVERNING DESIRES IN *AGNES GREY*

1. See Alice Renton, *Tyrant or Victim? A History of the British Governess* (London: Weidenfeld and Nicolson, 1991, and Trev Broughton and Ruth Symes (eds), *The Governess: An Anthology*, (Stroud: Sutton, 1997).

2. See Pamela Horn, 'The Victorian Governess', *History of Education*, 18. 4 (1989), 333-44.

3. M. Jeanne Peterson, 'The Victorian Governess: Status Incongruence in Family and Society', in Martha Vicinus (ed.), *Suffer and be Still: Women in the Victorian Age* (Bloomington and London: Indiana University Press, 1972), 4.

4. Ibid., 6.

5. Horn, 'The Victorian Governess', 333.

6. Peterson, 'The Victorian Governess', 11.

7. See Joan N. Burstyn, *Victorian Education and the Ideal of Womanhood* (New Jersey: Barnes and Noble, 1980), and Felicity Hunt (ed.), *Lessons for Life: The Schooling of Girls and Women, 1850–1950* (Oxford and New York: Blackwell, 1987).

8. See Laurie Langbauer, *Women and Romance: The Consolations of Gender in the English Novel* (New York: Cornell University Press, 1990).

9. Elizabeth Langland, *Anne Brontë: The Other One* (Basingstoke: Macmillan, 1989), 115.

10. Jill L. Matus, *Unstable Bodies: Victorian Representations of Sexuality and Maternity* (Manchester and New York: Manchester University Press, 1995), 92.

11. Langland, *Anne Brontë*, 106.

12. An interesting account of Anne Brontë's own solution to the problem of the intractable children who were placed in her charge during her time as a governess for the Inghams of Blake Hall comes from one of their descendants who recalls: 'In her old age Mrs. Ingham told one of her grandchildren that she had once employed

a very unsuitable governess called Miss Brontë who had actually tied the two children to a table leg in order to get on with her own writing. On entering the schoolroom the mother had been met by this horrifying sight and, of course, the governess had been suitably reprimanded.' Susan Brooke, 'Anne Brontë at Blake Hall', *Brontë Society Transactions*, 13: 68 (1958), 247.

13. For a more detailed account of inscriptions of class and colonialism in Brontë's language see Susan Meyer, 'Words on "Great Vulgar Sheets": Writing and Social Resistance in Anne Brontë's *Agnes Grey* (1847)', in Barbara Leah Harman and Susan Meyer (eds), *The New Nineteenth Century: Feminist Readings of Underread Victorian Fiction* (New York and London: Garland, 1996), 3–16.

14. Matus, *Unstable Bodies*, 93.

15. Meyer, 'Words on "Great Vulgar Sheets"', 13.

16. Ibid., 14.

CHAPTER 2. SPATIAL POLITICS IN *THE TENANT OF WILDFELL HALL*

1. Anne Brontë, 'Preface to the Second Edition', *TWH* 3.

2. Unsigned review, *Spectator*, 8 July 1848, 662–3; *CH* 250.

3. Unsigned review, *Athenaeum*, 8 July 1848, 670–71; *CH* 251.

4. E. P. Whipple, 'Novels of the Season', *North American Review*, October 1848, 354–69; *CH* 261.

5. Unsigned review, *Sharpe's London Magazine*, August 1848, 181–4; *CH* 263.

6. Ibid., *CH* 264.

7. Unsigned review, 'Mr Bell's New Novel', *Rambler*, September 1848, 65–6; *CH* 267–8.

8. Charles Kingsley, from an unsigned review, *Fraser's Magazine*, April 1849, 417–32; *CH* 271.

9. Ibid., *CH* 270.

10. Ibid., *CH* 271.

11. Terry Eagleton, *Myths of Power: A Marxist Reading of the Brontës* (London and Basingstoke: Macmillan, 1975), 136.

12. Ibid., 137.

13. Anthony Easthope and Kate McGowan (eds), *A Critical and Cultural Theory Reader* (Buckingham: Open University Press, 1992), 67.

14. See Mary Poovey, *Uneven Developments: The Ideological Work of Gender in Mid-Victorian England* (Chicago: The University of Chicago Press, 1988); Nina Auerbach, *Romantic Imprisonment: Women and Other Glorified Outcasts* (New York: Columbia University Press, 1985);

Deborah Gorham, *The Victorian Girl and the Feminine Ideal* (London: Croom Helm, 1982), and Lynda Nead, *Myths of Sexuality: Representations of Women in Victorian Britain* (Oxford: Blackwell, 1988).

15. Jan B. Gordon, 'Gossip, Diary, Letter, Text: Anne Brontë's Narrative *Tenant* and the Problematic of the Gothic Sequel', *English Literary History*, 51: 4 (1984), 719.

16. Unsigned review, *Examiner*, 29 July 1848, 483–4; CH 255.

17. Lori A. Paige, 'Helen's Diary Freshly Considered', *Brontë Society Transactions*, 20: 4 (1991), 226.

18. Gordon, 'Gossip, Diary, Letter, Text', 731.

19. Elizabeth Langland, 'The Voicing of Desire in Anne Brontë's *The Tenant of Wildfell Hall*', in Antony H. Harrison and Beverley Taylor (eds), *Gender and Discourse in Victorian Literature and Art* (Dekalb: Northern Illinois University, Press, 1992), 111.

20. Ibid., 115.

21. Laura C. Berry, 'Acts of Custody and Incarceration in *Wuthering Heights* and *The Tenant of Wildfell Hall*', *Novel*, 30: 1 (1996), 52.

22. John Sutherland, *Is Heathcliff a Murderer? Puzzles in 19th-Century Fiction* (Oxford: Oxford University Press, 1996), 73–7. Sutherland's discussion of naming in *The Tenant* raises the possibility that Helen is illegitimate.

23. Berry, 'Acts of Custody and Incarceration', 39.

24. See P. J. M. Scott, *Anne Brontë: A New Critical Assessment* (London: Vision Press, 1983).

25. Janet Kunert, 'Borrowed Beauty and Bathos: Anne Brontë, George Eliot, and "Mortification"', *Research Studies*, 46 (1978), 239–40.

CHAPTER 3.   A POETICS OF LOSS

1. Isobel Armstrong, *Victorian Poetry: Poetry, Poetics and Politics* (London and New York: Routledge, 1993), 324.

2. Unsigned review, *Critic*, 4 July 1846, 6–8; CH 59–60.

3. Chitham, *PAB*, 30.

4. Armstrong, *Victorian Poetry*, 339.

5. Elizabeth Langland, *Anne Brontë: The Other One* (Basingstoke: Macmillan, 1989), 88.

6. P. J. M. Scott, *Anne Brontë: A New Critical Assessment* (London: Vision Press, 1983), 52. Scott uses this expression in relation to 'Music on Christmas Morning'.

7. Maria Frawley, *Anne Brontë* (New York: Twayne, 1996), 49.

8. Chitham, *PAB*, 30.

9. Armstrong, *Victorian Poetry*, 333.

Select Bibliography

WORKS BY ANNE BRONTË

The Poems of Anne Brontë: A New Text and Commentary, ed. Edward Chitham (London and Basingstoke, Macmillan, 1979). An essential edition of the poems.

The Tenant of Wildfell Hall, ed. with an introduction and notes by Stevie Davies (London and New York: Penguin, 1986).

Agnes Grey, ed. with an introduction and notes by Angeline Goreau (London and New York: Penguin, 1988).

BIOGRAPHY

Barker, Juliet, *The Brontës* (London: Weidenfeld and Nicolson, 1994). A formidable account of the lives of the Brontës. Detailed, scholarly, compelling.

Chitham, Edward, *A Life of Anne Brontë* (Oxford and Cambridge, MA: Blackwell, 1991). An informed and balanced view of Brontë's life and work.

Gérin, Winifred, *Anne Brontë* (London: Allen Lane, 1959). Limited by its emphasis on the autobiographical aspects of Brontë's work.

Harrison, Ada and Derek Stanford, *Anne Brontë: Her Life and Work* (London: Methuen, 1959). An interesting attempt to assert Brontë's value as the first female realist writer.

CRITICAL WORKS

Allott, Miriam (ed.), *The Brontës: The Critical Heritage* (London and Boston: Routledge and Kegan Paul, 1974). A collection of reviews and criticism which provides insight into the contemporary literary context in which the Brontës worked.

Armstrong, Isobel, *Victorian Poetry: Poetry, Poetics and Politics* (London and New York: Routledge, 1993). A fascinating account of nine-teenth-century poetry with an indispensable chapter on women's writing.

Bell, Craig A., 'Anne Brontë: A Re-Appraisal', *Quarterly Review*, 304 (1966), 315–21. An overly defensive and somewhat quirky apprecia-tion of the novelist.

Berg, Margaret Mary, '*The Tenant of Wildfell Hall*: Anne Brontë's *Jane Eyre*', *Victorian Newsletter*, 71 (1987), 10–15. A concise account of the critical reception of Brontë's text and its relation to *Jane Eyre*.

Berry, Laura C., 'Acts of Custody and Incarceration in *Wuthering Heights* and *The Tenant of Wildfell Hall*', *Novel*, 30: 1 (1996), 32–55. A challenging account of the text which is informed by social and historical background as well as the work of Michel Foucault.

Brooke, Susan, 'Anne Brontë at Blake Hall', *Brontë Society Transactions*, 13: 68 (1958), 239–50. A biographical account of Brontë's governes-sing experiences which is attentive to the specific familial and regional culture in which Brontë found herself.

Costello, Priscilla H., 'A New Reading of Anne Brontë's *Agnes Grey*', *Bronte Society Transactions*, 19 (1986), 113–18. A brief account of how Brontë seeks to represent different classes within the novel.

Frawley, Maria, *Anne Brontë* (New York: Twayne, 1996). A detailed and considered feminist account of Brontë's work.

Gordon, Jan B., 'Gossip, Diary, Letter, Text: Anne Brontë's Narrative *Tenant* and the Problematic of the Gothic Sequel', *English Literary History*, 51: 4 (1984), 719–45. A subtle but sometimes misinformed reading of the novel.

Jackson, Arlene M., 'The Question of Credibility in Anne Brontë's *The Tenant of Wildfell Hall*', *English Studies*, 63: 3 (1982), 198–206. Helpful in its focus on Gilbert Markham's transformation into a convincing partner for Helen.

Jacobs, N. M., 'Gendered and Layered Narrative in *Wuthering Heights* and *The Tenant of Wildfell Hall*', *Journal of Narrative Technique*, 16: 3 (1986), 204–19. Perhaps the most detailed reading of Anne Brontë's narrative strategies.

Kunert, Janet, 'Borrowed Beauty and Bathos: Anne Brontë, George Eliot, and "Mortification"', *Research Studies*, 46 (1978), 237–47. An illuminating analysis of the significance of deathbed scenes in the works of both Brontë and Eliot.

Langland, Elizabeth, *Anne Brontë: The Other One* (Basingstoke: Macmillan, 1989). Useful and stimulating.

Langland, Elizabeth, 'The Voicing of Desire in Anne Brontë's *The Tenant of Wildfell Hall*' in Antony H. Harrison and Beverley Taylor (eds), *Gender and Discourse in Victorian Literature and Art* (Dekalb: Northern

Illinois University Press, 1992), 111–23. Emphasizes the transgressive and potentially subversive aspects of narrative exchange in Brontë's text.

Matus, Jill L., *Unstable Bodies: Victorian Representations of Sexuality and Maternity* (Manchester and New York: Manchester University Press, 1995), 89–156. A detailed and fascinating account of Brontë's *Agnes Grey* and Elizabeth Gaskell's *Ruth*.

McMaster, Juliet, ' "Imbecile Laughter" and "Desperate Earnest" in *The Tenant of Wildfell Hall*', *Modern Language Quarterly*, 43: 4 (1982), 352–68. An interesting reading which argues that through its portrayal of male aristocrats, *The Tenant* represents a Victorian critique of Regency culture and values.

Meyer, Susan, 'Words on "Great Vulgar Sheets": Writing and Social Resistance in Anne Brontë's *Agnes Grey*' (1847), in Barbara Leah Harman and Susan Meyer (eds), *The New Nineteenth Century: Feminist Readings of Underread Victorian Fiction* (New York and London: Garland, 1996), 3–16. A useful reading of Anne Brontë's language and discourse.

Paige, Lori A., 'Helen's Diary Freshly Considered', *Brontë Society Transactions*, 20: 4 (1991), 225–7. A short but subtle account of *The Tenant*.

Scott, P. J. M., *Anne Brontë: A New Critical Assessment* (London: Vision Press, 1983). A highly subjective account of Brontë's work but one which provides some helpful contextual information.

Thormahlen, Marianne, 'The Villain of *Wildfell Hall*: Aspects and Prospects of Arthur Huntington', *Modern Language Review*, 88: 4 (1993), 831–41. A productive attempt to place Brontë's portrayal of Huntington within the context of nineteenth-century theology and science.

Index

Recent and Forthcoming Titles in the New Series of

WRITERS AND THEIR WORK

RECENT & FORTHCOMING TITLES

Title	Author
Peter Ackroyd	*Susana Onega*
Kingsley Amis	*Richard Bradford*
Anglo-Saxon Verse	*Graham Holderness*
Antony and Cleopatra	*Ken Parker*
As You Like It	*Penny Gay*
W.H. Auden	*Stan Smith*
Alan Ayckbourn	*Michael Holt*
J.G. Ballard	*Michel Delville*
Aphra Behn	*Sue Wiseman*
John Betjeman	*Dennis Brown*
Edward Bond	*Michael Mangan*
Anne Brontë	*Betty Jay*
Emily Brontë	*Stevie Davies*
A.S. Byatt	*Richard Todd*
Caroline Drama	*Julie Sanders*
Angela Carter	*Lorna Sage*
Geoffrey Chaucer	*Steve Ellis*
Children's Literature	*Kimberley Reynolds*
Caryl Churchill	*Elaine Aston*
John Clare	*John Lucas*
S.T. Coleridge	*Stephen Bygrave*
Joseph Conrad	*Cedric Watts*
Crime Fiction	*Martin Priestman*
John Donne	*Stevie Davies*
Carol Ann Duffy	*Deryn Rees Jones*
George Eliot	*Josephine McDonagh*
English Translators of Homer	*Simeon Underwood*
Henry Fielding	*Jenny Uglow*
E.M. Forster	*Nicholas Royle*
Elizabeth Gaskell	*Kate Flint*
The *Gawain* Poet	*John Burrow*
The Georgian Poets	*Rennie Parker*
William Golding	*Kevin McCarron*
Graham Greene	*Peter Mudford*
Hamlet	*Ann Thompson & Neil Taylor*
Thomas Hardy	*Peter Widdowson*
David Hare	*Jeremy Ridgman*
Tony Harrison	*Joe Kelleher*
William Hazlitt	*J. B. Priestley; R. L. Brett (intro. by Michael Foot)*
Seamus Heaney	*Andrew Murphy*
George Herbert	*T.S. Eliot (intro. by Peter Porter)*
Henrik Ibsen	*Sally Ledger*
Henry James – The Later Writing	*Barbara Hardy*
James Joyce	*Steven Connor*
Julius Caesar	*Mary Hamer*
Franz Kafka	*Michael Wood*
William Langland: *Piers Plowman*	*Claire Marshall*
King Lear	*Terence Hawkes*
Philip Larkin	*Laurence Lerner*
D.H. Lawrence	*Linda Ruth Williams*
Doris Lessing	*Elizabeth Maslen*
C.S. Lewis	*William Gray*
David Lodge	*Bernard Bergonzi*
Christopher Marlowe	*Thomas Healy*
Andrew Marvell	*Annabel Patterson*
Ian McEwan	*Kiernan Ryan*
Measure for Measure	*Kate Chedgzoy*

TITLES IN PREPARATION

Title	Author
Chinua Achebe	Nahem Yousaf
Pat Barker	Sharon Monteith
Samuel Beckett	Keir Elam
Elizabeth Bowen	Maud Ellmann
Charlotte Brontë	Sally Shuttleworth
Lord Byron	Drummond Bone
Cymbeline	Peter Swaab
Daniel Defoe	Jim Rigney
Charles Dickens	Rod Mengham
Early Modern Sonneteers	Michael Spiller
T.S. Eliot	Colin MacCabe
Brian Friel	Geraldine Higgins
Ivor Gurney	John Lucas
Henry V	Robert Shaughnessy
Geoffrey Hill	Andrew Roberts
Kazuo Ishiguro	Cynthia Wong
Ben Jonson	Anthony Johnson
John Keats	Kelvin Everest
Rudyard Kipling	Jan Montefiore
Charles and Mary Lamb	Michael Baron
Language Poetry	Alison Mark
Malcolm Lowry	Hugh Stevens
Macbeth	Kate McCluskie
Dennis Potter	Derek Paget
Religious Poets of the 17th Century	Helen Wilcox
Revenge Tragedy	Janet Clare
Richard III	Edward Burns
Siegfried Sassoon	Jenny Hartley
Mary Shelley	Catherine Sharrock
Stevie Smith	Martin Gray
Muriel Spark	Brian Cheyette
Gertrude Stein	Nicola Shaughnessy
Laurence Sterne	Manfred Pfister
Tom Stoppard	Nicholas Cadden
Jonathan Swift	Ian Higgins
The Tempest	Gordon McMullan
Tennyson	Seamus Perry
Derek Walcott	Stewart Brown
John Webster	Thomas Sorge
Edith Wharton	Janet Beer
Jeanette Winterson	Margaret Reynolds
Women Romantic Poets	Anne Janowitz
Women Writers of the 17th Century	Ramona Wray
Women Poets of the Mid 19th Century	Gill Gregory
Women Writers of the Late 19th Century	Gail Cunningham

RECENT & FORTHCOMING TITLES

Title	Author
A Midsummer Night's Dream	Helen Hackett
Vladimir Nabokov	Neil Cornwell
V. S. Naipaul	Suman Gupta
Walter Pater	Laurel Brake
Brian Patten	Linda Cookson
Harold Pinter	Mark Batty
Sylvia Plath	Elisabeth Bronfen
Jean Rhys	Helen Carr
Richard II	Margaret Healy
Dorothy Richardson	Carol Watts
John Wilmot, Earl of Rochester	Germaine Greer
Romeo and Juliet	Sasha Roberts
Christina Rossetti	Kathryn Burlinson
Salman Rushdie	Damian Grant
Paul Scott	Jacqueline Banerjee
The Sensation Novel	Lyn Pykett
P.B. Shelley	Paul Hamilton
Wole Soyinka	Mpalive Msiska
Edmund Spenser	Colin Burrow
J.R.R. Tolkien	Charles Moseley
Leo Tolstoy	John Bayley
Charles Tomlinson	Tim Clark
Anthony Trollope	Andrew Sanders
Victorian Quest Romance	Robert Fraser
Angus Wilson	Peter Conradi
Mary Wollstonecraft	Jane Moore
Women's Gothic	Emma Clery
Virginia Woolf	Laura Marcus
Working Class Fiction	Ian Haywood
W.B. Yeats	Edward Larrissy
Charlotte Yonge	Alethea Hayter